PENGUIN BOOKS

WHO SHOULD BE SLEEPING
IN YOUR BED – AND WHY

James Oliver qualified as a clinical psychologist after taking a degree in anthropology at Cambridge University. After three years' research at Brunel University he worked for six years at a London mental hospital. In recent years he has been a television producer and interviewer and has worked on educational series on childcare (for Granada and BBC television), sex (*Sex with Paula Yates* for Channel 4) and violence (*Men and Violence* for ITV London Weekend Television). He has interviewed a celebrity each week in 'Room 113' on two series of Channel 4's award-winning youth programme *Network 7*.

JAMES OLIVER

WHO SHOULD BE SLEEPING IN YOUR BED – AND WHY

PENGUIN BOOKS

PENGUIN BOOKS

Published by the Penguin Group
27 Wrights Lane, London W8 5TZ, England
Viking Penguin Inc., 40 West 23rd Street, New York, New York 10010, USA
Penguin Books Australia Ltd, Ringwood, Victoria, Australia
Penguin Books Canada Ltd, 2801 John Street, Markham, Ontario, Canada L3R 1B4
Penguin Books (NZ) Ltd, 182–190 Wairau Road, Auckland 10, New Zealand

Penguin Books Ltd, Registered Offices: Harmondsworth, Middlesex, England

First published 1988
10 9 8 7 6 5 4 3 2 1

Filmset in Linotron Plantin by
Rowland Phototypesetting Ltd,
Bury St Edmunds, Suffolk
Made and printed in Great Britain by
Cox and Wyman Ltd, Reading, Berks

CONTENTS

Acknowledgements   7
Preface *by Roy Hutchins*   9
Introduction   13

**PART I   THE WHO'S WHO OF RELATIONSHIPS:
A COMPLETE GUIDE TO THE NINE TYPES OF
SEXUAL PERSONALITY**

1 *The Dimensions of Sexual Personality*   27

2 *The Lust Dimension*   31
   Faithful lust: the Donor   36
   Unfaithful lust: the Splitter   41
   Third-party lust: the Snatcher   48

3 *The Insecurity Dimension*   56
   The Bully   60
   The Clinger   66

4 *The Dominance Dimension*   73
   The Big Boy   80
   The Wimp   84
   The Little Princess   91
   The Cosmo   97

5 *The Map of Your Sexual Landscape*   105

**PART II   PREDICTING INFIDELITY:
A COMPLETE GUIDE TO THE TWENTY-EIGHT
TYPES OF COUPLE**

6 *The Causes of Infidelity*   109
   Distorted desires on the lust dimension   110
   Irrational fears on the insecurity dimension   112
   Incompatibility on the dominance dimension   114
   League table of couples' vulnerability to infidelity   122

7   *The Twenty-eight Types of Couple*   124
    Donor and Splitter   124
    Bully and Bully   128
    Bully and Cosmo   131
    Splitter and Clinger   134
    Bully and Big Boy   139
    Splitter and Wimp   143
    Splitter and Cosmo   147
    Bully and Donor   152
    Splitter and Little Princess   155
    Splitter and Big Boy   159
    Donor and Cosmo   162
    Donor and Big Boy   166
    Big Boy and Cosmo   169
    Donor and Wimp   173
    Clinger and Little Princess   177
    Donor and Little Princess   180
    Clinger and Wimp   183
    Wimp and Little Princess   187
    Splitter and Bully   190
    Clinger and Clinger   194
    Bully and Wimp   198
    Bully and Little Princess   201
    Clinger and Donor   204
    Clinger and Bully   208
    Clinger and Cosmo   212
    Clinger and Big Boy   215
    Big Boy and Little Princess   218
    Wimp and Cosmo   221

ACKNOWLEDGEMENTS

Without Roy Hutchins this book would never have been written. He was its impetus and had many helpful ideas in its conception.

Thanks are also due to Elsie Buckenham who, as ever, typed and retyped it with much more than a typist's eye for errors and inconsistencies; to Ravi Mirchandani for putting it forward for publication and backing it; to my literary agent, Aramintha Whitley, for her very helpful suggestions and support; and to Lucy Astor for her assistance in rethinking it and in helping to make understandable the case histories that lie behind this book.

PREFACE
by Roy Hutchins

Let me tell you a story . . . There was once a woman who lived happily with a man. They were very much in love. Then one day the woman fell in love with another man. She loved two men. A sexual triangle emerged. The two men became bitter enemies. There were huge scenes. One year later, five months pregnant and at the end of her tether, she took her own life.

It is – is it not? – a simple tale of infidelity, a true story that never made a headline and that was destined to be buried along with its victim, a story that joins millions of other stories, more or less tragic, to be found in the catalogue of human despair listed under 'the Eternal Triangle'. What singles out this story, however, is that when I heard it I asked myself one simple question: 'Why does infidelity occur?'

I decided to seek expert advice. The answer might make an interesting subject for a television play. Several dozen phone calls led me to a clinical psychologist by the name of James Oliver, an expert in the field of human relationships. I explained my quest. He responded, 'I'll begin to investigate the subject. Come over tomorrow.'

We met at his home and took tea in his rather impressive library. 'It has been a more difficult question to answer than I thought,' he said. 'To tell the truth, you kept me up all night, trying to find anything that came even close to explaining the phenomenon. The nearest I've come to it is this.' He passed me a book that lay open at a chapter which read 'Contributions to the Psychology of Love by Sigmund Freud'. It was an obscure, little-known paper and very difficult for the lay person to understand. 'This is the key,' explained Oliver. 'No doubt work by other psychologists can be traced and, together with original research, a modern theory could be developed.'

'But are there no easy-to-read books on the subject?' I asked naively.

He replied that there were not.

'Have you ever written a book?' I ventured.

'Several,' he replied.

They all turned out to be theoretical books. He had never written one for the general public. He agreed to write one for me. The subject? Sexual compatibility.

We began to look into the whole nature of sexual relationships. We interviewed countless infidelity sufferers. He developed an easy-to-understand theory for those who are unhappy or unsure in their sexual relationships, a tool that they can use to analyse their problem. And it is a tool *anybody* can use, so that he or she may learn to love the person who is right for them.

I would never have imagined that James Oliver would have come up with such a book. With a book that defines types of sexual couples and tells you whether to keep your lover or to call it a day. With a book that gives you precise instructions about who is best for you if you or your partner are involved with someone else. But I am glad he has done so, if only because of the benefit to my own sexual life, for I am now happily in love and no longer live under the dark shadow of fear called infidelity. That is not to say that unfaithful thoughts never cross my mind: as a man who leads a public life, temptation is often placed in my way, but now I understand how often my desire is distorted and that it is simply not worth threatening my long-term relationship. And to make sure I retain such a healthy attitude I give myself and my lover regular check-ups with the personality tests. The basis of this book is easy: know thyself, and find someone who's right for you, otherwise you will end up wasting your life away, torn between two people or hanging on in the hope that things might work out. They rarely do.

Two years ago a woman died. Had they only known then

what is available for you to know now, a beautiful young woman would still have the best years of her life stretching before her, and a little child might have been starting his or her first term at playgroup.

INTRODUCTION

This book is intended to explain, not encourage, infidelity. Surveys of couples have consistently found that between 50 and 70 per cent of wives and between 60 and 70 per cent of husbands admit to having had affairs. Men and women everywhere are now, in the light of AIDS, thinking twice before leaping into an adulterous bed. Yet they still leap.

If this book helps a single couple to understand better the causes of infidelity, and to avoid an affair, it will have been worth while.

The person who sleeps in your bed should be someone who wants to be faithful to you and to whom you wish to be faithful. That person is in this book. Getting it right is important because almost always infidelity, and the sexual triangles it gives rise to, leads to tremendous emotional disturbance.

There you are, more or less happily settled as one of a couple. Then one of you starts sleeping with another person. Now there is the FAITHFUL, the UNFAITHFUL and the THIRD PARTY: a sexual triangle. And now comes the emotional chaos – intense frustration, misery, despair, jealousy. The tears begin to flow. 'Give him up or we're finished,' 'You don't own me,' 'I can't share you,' 'Come and live with me,' and so on and on until something has to give. The problems become obsessive. They consume every waking moment and invade your dreams. Maybe you'll lose both of them; maybe you've been used; maybe you're bitter at being discarded; maybe you're the last to know and the first to suffer. Perhaps all three of you have tried hard to be reasonable and to fight the jealousy in a loving way. Your friends offer shoulders to cry on, share similar experiences; advice is given into the small hours; the phone bill mounts up. But none of it does any good, and the torture continues. Just like the games of naughty children, it always ends in tears. At the finish the triangle has left in its wake a pile of mangled emotions and deep wounds that will take many years to heal; the scars are for life.

WHY DO *YOU* THINK IT HAPPENS?

What on earth possesses us to enter this inferno? Maybe you have the same sorts of idea that I had when I first considered the problem. Here's a simple quiz to test your knowledge of the most common causes of sexual infidelity. Answer TRUE or FALSE to the following statements.

One of the main motives for sexual infidelity is:		
Too much routine in a marriage – the 'seven-year itch'	TRUE	FALSE
Taking revenge on a partner	TRUE	FALSE
Secretaries seducing their bosses	TRUE	FALSE
Pepping up relationships by creating jealousy	TRUE	FALSE
The female menopause	TRUE	FALSE
The male menopause	TRUE	FALSE
Partners going on business trips	TRUE	FALSE
The attraction of someone of importance and high status	TRUE	FALSE
The chance to get a 'sugar daddy'	TRUE	FALSE
Getting too close to a friend	TRUE	FALSE
The corrupting influence of power	TRUE	FALSE
An older man seeking a younger woman	TRUE	FALSE
Basic physical, sexual lust	TRUE	FALSE

How many did you score as TRUE? Well, it may come as a surprise to you to learn the truth about these statements: *all of them are false*. They are simply modern folklore – myths, superstitious tales with which we blind ourselves. The truth is very different, and, as with all real truths, it is very, very simple.

SEXUAL MYTHOLOGIES

Let us take one of the commonest of these myths and expose it to proper scrutiny: the 'seven-year itch'.

It is widely held that the dynamic forces at work in any marriage come into a state of conflict after a period of about seven years. This disjunction creates a stasis in which the original play of energy between the couple has become locked into a stalemate. In order to create some movement in this gummed-up marital fishpond, so the theory goes, one of the couple expresses his or her boredom and restlessness by taking a lover.

Not only is this hypothesis needlessly complex in its predicates but, far more important, it is quite simply *not true* – the great majority of marriages end, or are the victims of infidelity, in the *third* year, not the seventh. Anyway a far simpler explanation exists for what is known as the 'seven-year itch', which we shall come to presently.

Or, again, consider the myth that money can be the main cause of infidelity. Here the argument is that a discrepancy in wealth between two people creates the conditions in which a sexual relationship develops. The poorer individual needs more money, or would prefer a more affluent lifestyle, or would like both at the same time. The richer party is prepared to exchange riches for the sexual favours – and possibly, in some cases, even love – that the poorer one is prepared to give in return. A complex commercial transaction is proposed, rather like the byzantine dealings that take place in stock exchanges all over the world.

But, of course, it is obvious that this over-complicated 'explanation' explains nothing. In its long-winded way all that this jumped-up theory does is to note the obvious fact that economic inequality between partners exists and then to offer this fact as the reason why they become lovers. As we shall see, money is usually not, in itself, the cause of sexual infidelity.

But the 'seven-year itch' and the 'money' theories appear

positively simplistic when laid beside the tortuous twists of logic that must be followed if we are to adopt the 'lust' theory. In this case we are required to absorb a mass of anatomical and stylistic detail that, it is held, are the basis for the attraction between the two individuals in question. It is her breasts, skin, eyes, flat stomach, behind, sinuous way of walking and so forth – not to mention her mini-skirt, brightly coloured T-shirts, scarves, socks, shoes (before we get to her make-up, sweet-smelling perfume, tinted hair and so on) – that, taken altogether, are what attract him to her; while she is attracted to his muscular legs and shoulders, his behind, his chest, his freewheeling gait, his tight trousers, tasteful shirts and jackets, splendid choice in footwear, his hairstyle, fragrant aftershave, anti-perspirant, etc., etc.

Surely matters need not be so complex? And yet those are just the premises of the theory. For now, on the one hand, we are forced to examine still 'deeper' and more 'fundamental' factors in analysing sexual attraction, like the chemistry of sexuality (with all the evidence about hormones, imprinting and secretions from improbable parts of the body), and, on the other hand, we must listen to lectures on the sociology of sex, the anthropology of sex, the psychology of sex, 'the use of language in sexual encounters', until by the end of it all we have forgotten what subject we were thinking about, let alone the question we were asking. But, really, does something so natural and so normal and so simple as sexual love between two people need to be turned into such a mystery? Our answer is a resounding *no*, and the time has come to show that the infidelity that causes so much unhappiness is understandable in terms of a few simple, even obvious, truths. It's time to get back to the basics.

THE THREE BASIC REQUIREMENTS FOR SEXUAL INFIDELITY

Stripped down to their bare elements, three conditions are necessary and always present when any act of sexual infidelity takes place.

Problems in the original couple

Something is *missing*, and there are negative, dissatisfying aspects *present* in the relationship. This creates an openness to infidelity, or an active seeking of it by one partner, as the couple tries to escape the frustration or seek out what is missing.

A preparedness to be unfaithful

One of the partners must be of a kind who will use infidelity, rather than some other means, as the solution to his or her difficulties.

A third party who is willing and able

There must be someone who either actively seeks the potentially unfaithful partner or is a willing recipient of his or her attention. This person must also appeal to the potentially unfaithful partner as someone who will provide what's missing and who will not simply reproduce the unhappiness of the original couple.

Put as simply as possible, then, infidelity takes place when a couple aren't getting on well and one of them tries to find the solution with a new lover who is willing to give it a go. But putting it like that begs as many questions as it answers. It does not, for example, rule out any of the 'myths' listed above – any of them could be used to explain why the unfaithful is unhappy or seeks another lover. The key question becomes:

WHY DO PEOPLE GET ALONG WELL OR BADLY IN SEXUAL RELATIONSHIPS?

Many factors determine how people get on. Looks, class, wealth, culture, intelligence: the list of things that we look for *initially* in another person is seemingly endless. But, having said that, there are only three factors that are absolutely crucial once a relationship has started. The fundamental reasons why we get on well can be summarized as follows.

Compatibility

If you're not compatible, it's a big problem. Compatibility has three key aspects. First, the compatibility of your *styles of aggression*. Two people who are very forceful and dominating will clash. One of you needs to be prepared to concede to the other. Secondly, compatible *values*. The two of you must see eye to eye in your basic philosophies of life. That doesn't mean, for example, that politically right-wing and left-wing people will never get on, but unless your basic beliefs about right and wrong, about how to live your life, about what really matters, are suited, there is bound to be trouble. Thirdly, compatible ideas about *sexual identity*. That doesn't mean how you like to have sex and what you think about it – although obviously these are important; it means that you must both feel happy with each other's ideas about the sort of man or woman that you like – the way you both go about expressing your gender. For example, a woman who wants a partner with the traditional male characteristics is going to have trouble with one who questions them and vice versa.

Security in relationships

Ideally, both of you bring to the relationship the expectation that when you get close to people they will be reliable and loving and able to fulfil your needs. Each partner is 'innocent until proved guilty' if both are secure in their way of relating. The expectation is that you won't be let down and that your partner can, and will, give you what you need. Only when he or she actually lets you down do you complain. Unfortunately, all too many people bring to their relationships mistrust, suspicion and a fear of being cheated and deceived *even when there is no reason to expect those things*. Treating people as if they have let you down when they haven't breeds further mistrust and leads to friction.

Realistic lust

To get on well, your desire for each other needs to be just that: a desire *for each other*, for the actual face, body and personality that each of you has and not for those of a fantasy figure out of your dreams. Many people desire an imaginary partner; not surprisingly, it upsets them when the reality intrudes upon the fantasy – 'You're not the woman I married,' 'You've changed.' No, the partner hasn't changed. He or she still looks the same. It's the fantasy that's changed (or ended). Just as we hear what we want to hear (which is not necessarily the same as what people say to us), so we are liable to see the objects of desire that we want to see. When we first meet people we often 'invent' them, and it can take years to recognize the difference between the reality and the fantasy. Using models from our past, we are prone to 'constructing' our lovers. This means we get on badly when the truth of the present reality becomes apparent to us. To get on well, both partners must desire what the other actually is like.

To put it the other way round, then, people get on badly in sexual relationships because of one or more of the following three reasons: incompatibility; an irrational fear of being let down; and distorted, unrealistic desire. Lots of other things come into it, of course, but basically it's as simple as that. The causes are not money, age, jealousy, being 'over-sexed', milkmen or any of the hundred and one other folktales that have been doing the rounds (each with their grain of truth).

THE GAP

In my researches I have come upon one particular phenomenon over and over again, to which I have given a name. I call it the Gap.

When people are intensely involved with each other there is a tremendous amount at stake emotionally. There are always thoughts and feelings – realities – that cannot be faced. Rather than live with these unbearable realities, people prefer to tell themselves and each other a story. There is the jilted lover who blames it all on his or her partner, the couple whose relationship is riddled with dissatisfaction and is obviously without a future (obviously to everyone except them, that is – 'We have our problems, but there's a special something that keeps us together,' they say, yet they admit to you in private moments and with brief, soon forgotten flashes of honesty that this is nonsense, a myth they propagate to ward off the truth) or the lovers who heap blame on themselves for what is going wrong rather than doing something constructive about it when blame is irrelevant. There are no limits to the ingenuity and skill employed by people engaged in this work of self-deception.

Between what people involved in sexual relationships really feel and what they tell themselves, each other and anyone who will support what they believe lies the Gap, the gulf between the reality of the relationship and the story they have made up about it. Only by bridging that gulf can we achieve satisfying relationships.

The fictional side of the Gap is drawn largely from popular culture. Society provides stock plots for imaginary melodramas. There is a set of phrases, verbal formulae, that provide the clichéd lines for the speeches of lovers. 'It's all over,' 'He means everything to me,' 'We were so much in love,' 'There's been nobody else,' 'I've been true to him,' and on and on – the phrases slip out like a never-ending episode from hackneyed romantic fiction or the chorus from a pop song. The language is clichéd because the sentiments that it expresses are untrue. You can always tell when people have crossed to the other side of the Gap: their speech becomes far more realistic: 'We love each other because we both *trust* each other, and we trust each other because we know that we'd never abuse our intimacy.'

And the plots. There are many variants, but they usually come down to one of the basic scenarios that start with the fairytales of childhood and continue on television and in films in later life. Someone is GOOD (usually me) and someone else is BAD (usually you or a competitor for you). Or someone has been behaving in a MAD way (not me, nearly always you) and someone else is SANE ('Thank God one of us is sane – i.e. me.

You're so crazy'). Or sometimes someone has been MAD but GOOD while someone else is SANE but BAD. Mental health or morality provide the basis for most of the plots. Along with such things as attractiveness, wealth, status, deviousness and power, these qualities are thought to be responsible for what happens to us in our sexual relationships. And we use the language of the pop song and the fictional melodrama to tell these stories to ourselves and each other.

On the other side of the Gap is the reality of what has happened.

A classic example of the Gap

It seems so self-evident as hardly to require explanation that an older married man should desire a younger woman. On the one hand, you've got a wife whose skin is beginning to wrinkle, whose hips and behind have been enlarged by child-bearing, whose breasts are beginning to sag, who's putting on weight, whose clothing is correspondingly discreet and designed as much to conceal disadvantageous features as to draw attention to sexy ones, who is familiar, perhaps nagging, perhaps depressed and probably hard-pressed to say something you've never heard before. And, on the other hand, there is the sexy younger woman: clear-skinned, dressed to kill rather than to sedate, firm-breasted, slim-hipped, pert, alive, perhaps amusing, perhaps full of fun, probably dead keen on sex, and she finds you attractive in a way you haven't experienced since . . . you first met your wife. Surely few things in life could be easier to explain than this affair. There's no contest. It's the story of the beauty and the beast.

Well, it *does* take a lot of explaining. For example, most men will find the younger woman more desirable in this situation, but by no means all of them will act on this desire if opportunity knocks. On the contrary, many will not touch her. *How do you explain the fact that some men do and some don't, if the only reason is the younger woman's superior physical attractions?*

And what about the younger woman's behaviour? Let's see how you're going to explain her. On the one hand there is available a paunchy, middle-aged man with a thousand commitments and an incapacity to understand half the words she uses because he's so out of touch with her age group's culture and, on the other, any of the dozens of svelte, smooth and sophisticated young men that chat her up day in, day out, all year long. No doubt you've got all the standard replies ready. She likes his reliability, money, 'maturity' and all the rest of it. But is that really why she does it?

Let's see what they tend to say.

He says: 'I was getting tired of *the old ball and chain*. *Seven-year itch, call it what you will*. I loved her, of course I did, she and the kids, *they were my whole world*. But *something was missing*, that *extra something*, you know, *that spark which makes all the difference*. And then I met her [the younger woman]. *Of course I'd fancied other women before*, but her, *there was something special about her*. I mean, of course, she looked fantastic, *a real corker*. *I fancied her something rotten*. But it wasn't only that. Honestly, it wasn't. *It was her youthful innocence*. It made such a change from the *routine grind* of *my nine-to-five existence*. *I couldn't help myself*. *It just happened*.'

His wife says: 'She was a *devious little bitch*. She seduced him with her *tarty way* of *carrying on*. *She gave it to him on a plate*, and he found it irresistible. The selfish, *loose little tart* couldn't care less; *his scarlet woman*, she's *very generous with her favours*. *It's all over the office*. *She can't say no to anyone wearing trousers*. She's a calculating *little vixen*.'

The younger woman says: '*He wasn't like the others*. He had *maturity*. *He was a real gentleman*, not just a case of "*wham-bam-thank-you-mam*". He wasn't going *to use me*. *He knew how to treat a girl*. And it *made me feel good* to be *shown some respect*. Not that I didn't fancy him. He was *a real good-looker* in his own *quiet sort of way*. *The dark, silent type*, you know.'

I have emphasized clichéd or empty expressions that are employed as a substitute for a real attempt to find the exact words to describe their unique experiences. The three speeches are typical of the kind of accounts that I have been given by people in these circumstances. I have not exaggerated the extent to which the language is flat and derivative. These people are telling themselves a story to conceal the reality. They are stuck on the wrong side of the Gap, and the language that they are employing prevents them from crossing any bridges to the other side.

And then there are the plots of the tales they are telling. He says he loves his wife but that there was 'something missing'. No doubt he is right about that, but he makes little attempt to identify what it is. He feels that the affair was a contrast to his 'nine-to-five existence', but he attaches most importance to something called her 'youthful innocence'. It's almost as if he's trying to persuade us that it was only lust that really motivated him, so weak are the other motives that he offers.

His wife's account is not much more convincing. She's angry, and she blames the younger woman rather than her husband. She resorts to painting the 'other woman' red in an attempt to run her down – trying to link her in our minds with a woman who has sex for money, a prostitute. Do you believe her or, for that matter, her husband? It's not that they're deliberately lying, but don't you get the feeling that they're telling themselves convenient stories?

The younger woman's story is that she was charmed by the middle-aged man's courtly manners and gentlemanly conduct – not that she would have us believe she didn't find him sexually attractive, mark you. On the contrary, he was the 'dark, silent type', a 'real good-looker' in a 'quiet sort of way'. Is she talking about the real person with whom she made love or a character out of romantic fiction?

The reality of the classic 'middle-aged man, his wife and a sexy younger woman' story varies, but it always comes down to some combination of incompatibility, irrational fear and distorted lust that creates problems for the original couple, a preparedness to be unfaithful and a third party who fits the bill and is able and willing to do so.

*

If you're a member of a couple, regardless of whether infidelity has occurred, the chances are that the Gap exists to some degree in your case: it's very likely that neither you nor your partner is fully aware of the true reasons why you get on well or badly. The basic building blocks of the bridge for crossing the Gap are provided in Part I of this book. I have identified nine types of sexual personality and profiles, and diagnostic tests for these personalities are provided. The sooner you get to work, the better. If it hasn't done so already, your relationship could slide over the precipice and fall into the pit of infidelity. If you're already in the pit, I'm throwing you a rope ladder – and from the side of reality, not fantasy.

PART I

The Who's Who of Relationships: a Complete Guide
to the Nine Types of Sexual Personality

1 THE DIMENSIONS OF SEXUAL PERSONALITY

The purpose of this part is to enable you to identify your sexual personality type and tendencies, and those of your lover (or the other participants if you're in a sexual triangle). It's crucial for you to do this, whether you're single or a member of a couple or of a triangle. Once you know your type you'll be able to establish which partner is right for you, what the risks of infidelity are and what to do in any sexual triangles that occur.

We have already mentioned the three fundamental issues in any sexual relationship: lust, insecurity and dominance. The chapters in this part of the book analyse your personality type with regard to each of them.

These issues are not equally important in everyone. Dominance may be central for one person, whereas insecurity may be the driving force for another. The fact that one issue is more important doesn't mean that the others don't matter. All three issues affect everyone to some extent. We call these issues *dimensions of sexual personality*. Anyone involved in a sexual relationship has all three dimensions operating simultaneously.

Dimensions have extremes at either end, and people vary according to where they are located between them. For instance, at one end of the dominance dimension is dominance and at the other end submissiveness. In sexual relationships some people tend to be dominant and would therefore take their place at one end of the scale, while others tend to be submissive and will therefore come at the the other end of the scale. The end that you occupy defines the *personality type* that you have with respect to this dimension: everyone is more or less dominant and therefore has a personality type on the dominance dimension.

What we have just said goes for the insecurity and lust dimensions too. Everyone has tendencies with regard to insecurity and lust in sexual relationships. However, just as there is a hierarchy of importance of the dimensions for each person, so it is with the personality types: everyone has one personality type which is more important than the others. This is called the *sexual personality type* (or SPT for short). The tendencies you have with respect to the other two dimensions are called the *second* and *third tendencies*.

Now, the chances are that you dislike the idea that you can be pigeon-holed as one sort of person, and perhaps it's worth clarifying the notion of 'personality type' a bit. People are immensely complex and sophisticated, and it must be admitted that sticking labels on them always involves an over-simplification.

Take the dominance dimension. Nobody tends *only* to be dominant in his or her relationships; everyone is submissive sometimes. And people can be largely dominant in one relationship, yet largely submissive in another that is going on at the same time. Or you might be dominant for a few months and then gradually become submissive in the same relationship. Also you might dominate in some situations with your lover (say, in bed) and be totally submissive in others (say, in all matters relating to travel, like choosing routes and hotels on holiday or directions when looking for a cinema on a night out). And not only are *you* complex but *so is your lover*! Everyone's personality can vary from time to time, from situation to situation.

However, having said all that (and I could say a lot more), the fact is that people do have consistent and distinctive patterns of thinking and feeling and of behaving. These patterns date back to childhood and are in each person's unique make-up. However much it might not seem so, when you take a broad look at any individual's behaviour over time, and in a wide variety of circumstances, regularities emerge.

It is because of these regularities that it's possible to identify types of personality. (For example, in any couple dominance and submission arise continually as issues. No couple agrees about everything, so there will always be conflicts. In the end, someone has got to give way. Some people give way more easily than others: that's the type of people they are.) So if you dislike the idea that you fit into a category, a type, try to think whether there are any patterns to your behaviour. Haven't you got to admit that there are? If there weren't, you'd be totally chaotic and unpredictable, a different person from one moment to the next. Well, you're not (unless you're mad!), and that's because you have a regular personality. And that personality is one of a type.

Identifying your SPT is the key to analysing it. In addition, if you are involved in a sexual triangle, you must identify the SPT of both the other participants. Only when these have been identified is it possible to establish the causes of the infidelity and to give clear indications as to what is best for each participant.

The first step is to establish where you and any other participants are located on the lust, the insecurity and the dominance dimensions in the chapters that follow. For each personality type there is a diagnostic test, and if you are persistent and honest, you should have no problems in establishing the SPT of all the participants on all three dimensions.

What to do if you're in a sexual triangle but you don't know one of the participants. If you're involved in a triangle but do not know one of the participants, you'll obviously find it difficult to identify his or her personality type. For instance, if you're faithful but have an unfaithful partner who refuses to tell you anything about the third party, you've got a problem. My advice is – it's time you found out about this stranger. When it comes to triangles ignorance is not bliss, and you're only fooling yourself if you pretend that you'd rather not know. You've got to become a detective. You've got to seek out any clues to the personality of this shadowy figure. Search your lover's pockets; read his or her personal diaries; root around in all possible hiding places for those crucial lover's letters; ask friends of your lover to divulge their sworn secrets. Any means will justify the end. Remember, you're probably the last person to know (if you're a faithful), so there are almost certainly people at work or in your social circle who can provide the information you so badly need. Do not feel any guilt about doing this – it's for the good of your lover as well as yourself. Your life is being affected by this state of affairs, and you've a right to know – in fact, the future of your love life depends on it.

And my advice to any third party who is ignorant about the faithful partner is the same: stop at nothing to discover what type of person he or she is. You know where your lover lives: spy on the couple or refuse your lover sexual pleasures until you are told some scraps about the faithful partner. Turn it into a game, or do it in earnest. Just find out.

2 THE LUST DIMENSION

Before I explain how lust works in couples, it's time to do the first diagnostic test to find out where you are on the lust dimension. *It's essential that you do the test before reading what follows.*

To diagnose your personality type, take a clean sheet of paper and write the numbers 1–20 down the left-hand side. To each question answer 'yes' or 'no'.

1. At the moments when you feel warmth and love for a partner you rarely also feel lust for him or her.
2. You don't get jealous if your partner goes out with people of your own sex.
3. You like to vary the places where you have sex with a steady love.
4. You do not feel that it's necessarily the end of the world (or your relationship) if your partner has an affair.
5. You quite fancy the idea of having affairs or casual involvements alongside your main relationship.
6. If you see your partner being chatted up, it doesn't bother you at all.
7. You tend to blow hot and cold during foreplay and intercourse, and you are turned on and off within short periods.
8. You are critical and doubtful about your ability to satisfy your partner and tend to believe that other people would be more able to do so.
9. You often feel critical of people to whom you're attracted; immediately after intercourse you often feel uneasy and unrelaxed.
10. You're the sort of person who'd be the last to know if your partner had an affair.
11. You think that sex is a bit wicked and dirty, and

sometimes you feel that you or your partner are degraded by it.

12. You find it hard to admit to yourself that you feel possessive about your partner.

13. At work you fear, yet admire, your boss.

14. Often there is one person of the opposite sex in your life whom you fancy but don't respect, perhaps privately, and another to whom you feel very close but don't fancy.

15. You can conceive that if your partner had an affair, your own sex life together would improve.

16. It's important to you to have sex a lot.

17. You are very concerned indeed about dirty living accommodation or bad personal hygiene (your own and others) or untidiness or nasty smells.

18. MEN: Women are either angelic and wonderful, or else you fancy them rotten as sex objects, but no one woman is both at the same time.

    WOMEN: Men are attractive and exciting to you because they're cruel or unavailable or else they are 'really nice' but you 'just don't fancy them'.

19. You are very helpful in seeing what's best for others but unable to do this for yourself.

20. You think sex is a pretty physical thing and, in the end, that you can't beat a good screw for getting rid of frustrations.

Before finding out your score and making your diagnosis (see page 47), you must read the following introduction to the lust dimension and the profiles of the first two lust personality types, the faithful and the unfaithful.

'Sex, that's what sexual infidelity is all about,' you might think. Well, not only are dominance and insecurity at least as important, but also the part that lust plays is far more complex than you might first think.

To begin with, you've got to consider why people fancy each other. It's not obvious. Think of some of the people your friends desire – you don't fancy them at all! Again, ask yourself why you prefer men with long legs or blondes rather than brunettes and so on. You have to admit that it's not because people with these characteristics are in any way 'objectively' sexier. It's just down to your personal preferences. So where do these preferences come from? What is the cause of sexual chemistry?

Society says that some shapes and sizes are sexier than others. OK. But if you line up fifty people who meet society's specification for sexiness, everyone will have his or her own preferences – the fifty people won't all seem equally desirable. And in explaining their preferences people would list personality characteristics, as well as physical ones, as important, even though they have never met any of these sexual objects. So it's not just what someone looks like that causes lust; for everyone there is a mix of physical and psychological attributes in others that is appealing.

These attributes are laid down in childhood. On the whole, men search for their mothers, and women their fathers, in their choice of lovers later on. But the choice is not necessarily straightforward. While some women may fancy only tall but retiring men because their fathers were tall and retiring, other women with similar fathers may choose men precisely because they are not like that. The key point is that, either way, preferences are *responses* to what parents of the opposite sex were like. (People are also affected by what their siblings were like.) It's not, so to speak, an independent choice, unaffected by the past.

The reason why it's all so complicated is that sex between family members is prohibited. You can't sleep with your mum or dad, your sister or brother. It's absolutely forbidden even to suggest that you might want to, let alone to make any moves in that direction. But that doesn't mean people don't want to. There'd be no need for an incest taboo if people didn't want to perform incest; there's no need to forbid something that people don't want to do. For example, there is no taboo against picking the noses or burning the clothes of fellow family members because there's no need: hardly

anyone wants to do these things! But people do have inces-
tuous wishes, and they are stamped on right from the start.
(We needn't go into the reasons here.)

And it is near the start of life that they are stamped on
because, from a very young age, children clearly demonstrate
a primitive, childish version of lust. Anyone who has seen an
ordinary 4-year-old girl with her father or a little boy of a
similar age with his mother would have to admit it. However,
for the little child there is no hope of success. Quite apart
from the physical impossibility of adult sex acts for people of
this age, children have to face the fact that there is an
adversary whom they cannot hope to compete with – their
mum (for girls) or dad (for boys). On top of this is the very
considerable disapproval and rejection which the child normally encounters from the adults at the slightest expression
of its desire.

So it's not on. But it's not on in very different ways,
varying from triangle to triangle. This is where the eternal
triangle has its roots – that's why it's eternal, as almost
everyone goes through this competition – and it is here that
each individual's basic triangular predispositions are laid
down. As a result of our particular childhood triangles there
are three possible positions we can assume in later life.

1. The faithful Donor

This is someone who gave up the struggle out of guilt or
hopelessness and said, 'I donate you to a more impressive
competitor.' They are boys who are giving mummy back to
daddy, accepting that he should get what is rightfully his.
And they are girls who give daddy to mummy in triangular
situations – they daren't put up a fight. In adult triangles
these people are always the faithful party whose lover has
been snatched away from them or who share their lover.

2. The unfaithful Splitter

This child's lust was so fiercely prohibited that he or she has
divided the world into people to be desired and people to be
loved. Such adults daren't lust after someone they love

because love for a familiar person brings back those terrifying threats of punishment with which their childish lust was greeted. They either romanticize or lust crudely after lovers in adult life, but once the lover becomes *familiar* (that is, like a family member), the desire wanes. Either they keep lovers at arm's length or the lust disappears. If that happens, they are very liable to start fancying third parties and to start seeking affairs. These people are always the unfaithful party in adult triangles.

3. The third-party Snatcher

This person didn't give up the fight and is still trying to snatch mummy from daddy (men) or daddy from mummy (women). They have not accepted defeat and, in later life, are prone to snatch lovers out of couples to gain a victory that eluded them in their childhood past. These people are always the third party in an adult triangle.

All of us are prone to one of these positions whether or not we have ever been a participant in a triangle where actual infidelity occurred. For some people it's easy to identify which they are: the secretary who always seems to end up with married men from work, or the man who has ended up several times sleeping with his best friend's girl – these are probably Snatchers. Likewise the men or women who always end up being unfaithful, however much they love their current partners – they're probably Splitters. The perpetual 'victim' husband or wife whose spouse is always unfaithful or the person who always seems to lose out to a more impressive competitor – they're most likely Donors.

For others it's not so obvious. Maybe this is the first actual triangle you've ever been in, so you can't identify any pattern in your behaviour. But, remember, almost everyone has been in an eternal triangle – the one with our parents – so you might find clues there. And remember Jimmy Carter's comment about having committed adultery in his heart: you don't have to experience life in a triangle to know where your predilections lie.

If you're one of a couple and want to know whether you are running the risk of a triangle, study the Donor and Splitter sections on the following pages in relation to yourself and your partner. It will help you to identify where the risk lies, and, ultimately, how to avoid it: whether you're a Donor or a Splitter you can fight this tendency alone and together.

FAITHFUL LUST: THE DONOR

Personality profile

Dimension: **Lust**

Type: **Donor**

Position in triangle: **The faithful**

Famous examples of this sexual personality type: Ken Barlow and Vera Duckworth (*Coronation Street*), Lucy Ewing (*Dallas*), Mrs Cecil Parkinson, Jackie Kennedy, Sue (Ali's wife in *EastEnders*)

General profile

Donors are broadminded types. They think seriously about their relationships for themselves and the people they love – even if this means certain painful choices. Some may say that they are intense, but Donors know that falling in love is not a thing to be taken lightly.

Some Donors want their partners to share their closest friendships. They don't want to become locked away in an exclusive relationship. So they'll encourage their partners to socialize with their friends because 'I'm sure you'll really get on. You've got a lot in common.' Such an open-minded, trusting attitude is, unfortunately, all too often abused, and the Donor's partner may repay this liberality with an act of infidelity.

Other Donors may sense that their partner is being 'chased' by someone else, but they won't cause a scene and will trust them to remain true. Again, sadly, this trust may be abused. These Donors' friends may say, 'You saw what was going on. You should have put up more of a fight,' but duels before breakfast are not their style, and they reply, 'My partner either loves me or not. A true relationship should exist without having to fight over a lover.'

Yet other Donors realize that their partner is not happy with them, and, out of a love that is far greater than most, they will suggest their lover should have an affair. At this the lover will normally remonstrate, 'But I don't want to. I'm quite happy with you,' but these Donors know that 'quite' is not good enough. They love their partner so much that they want them to be completely happy.

Before an affair develops, and especially if it is with a mutual friend, most Donors feel very impressed with the third party because they recognize in the person qualities which they themselves lack. Donors are the first to be self-critical in relationships; they are rarely smug (although their partners can think them self-righteous). They know their faults, and they realize that their competitor is supplying a need. However, they won't necessarily continue to feel this way once the affair is properly under way. Donors may see friends in a new light if they've been betrayed by them, and they can perceive faults as well as good points.

Donors really are always the last to know. Their innocent, trusting tendencies can lead them to turn a blind eye to what's going on. Once an affair starts, Donors are subject to great anxiety and, sometimes, intense depressions. Yet, surprisingly, sex with their unfaithful partner often markedly improves, as the air is cleared and things are said which have previously been bottled up. During the build-up to the affair, and in its early phases, Donors may throw themselves into their work, or a hobby, or a sport; deep down they know the relationship is on the rocks, and they try to keep it off their minds. Some Donors may drink heavily, or smoke more than usual, or even gamble as the pressure mounts up. It's not easy being a Donor; you often feel you're carrying the full weight of the relationship on your shoulders.

Donors have two main responses to an affair once it is well established. Some get deeply depressed and feel old, out of date, cast off like a worn-out shoe. Others may decide to win their lover back. They will smarten up their appearance (substitute contact lenses for glasses, get their hair restyled, buy new clothes) and enter into the competition with all the enthusiasm of a Snatcher (see p. 48).

At work some Donors always seem to be encouraging their colleagues to apply for promotion. They will even put in a good word to the boss (for whom these Donors usually feel intense respect and fear) on their behalf. This often results in their peers gaining promotion before them and the selfless Donor is left only with disillusionment and a feeling of being second-best, which is intensified when they realize, on reflection, that they could have done the job even better. It is typical of a Donor to put others first. Other Donors, however, are quicker to spot what's happening. Once it's sunk in, they fight tenaciously to get what is rightfully theirs.

Your Donor is a pacifist at heart, peace-loving and unaggressive. If someone gets angry or violent, the Donor is the first on the scene to placate and pour oil on troubled waters. If things do get violent, however, Donors become highly anxious – nervous, very tense, shaky. They never get violent themselves.

Open-minded and exploited, trusting and betrayed, loving and losing, selfless to the last – that's the Donor. Donors always want to give, and sometimes it's the thing most precious to them – the person they love.

The psychology of the Donor

Surveys in women's magazines invariably reveal that about half of all married housewives have had affairs. Another way of looking at that statistic is that half haven't. Fidelity is at least as widespread as infidelity!

We might ask, 'Why are people faithful?' Most people would admit, as Jimmy Carter did, to fancying people other than their lover. But this admission is a relatively new development. It was not long ago that adultery was so heavily frowned upon that it was dangerous to acknowledge the wish, let alone the reality. This view was powerfully supported by strict moral and religious ideas. Nowadays people would generally provide emotional rather than moral or religious reasons for fidelity: 'It's a matter of trust'; 'I hate the idea of him/her with another woman/man', 'It's not worth risking our relationship just for sex' and so on.

Whatever the positive reasons for preferring fidelity, there are a great many negative ones against *in*fidelity. The emotional and practical problems of sharing a lover are legion: envy, feelings of humiliation, insecurity about losing the partner, competition for his or her time (and these are but a few of them).

Given the advantages of fidelity and the numerous black marks against infidelity, it is surprising that anyone would actually *donate* a partner, more or less explicitly supporting the development of an affair. Yet, to some extent, this is precisely what happens in every triangle.

It will be objected immediately by some faithfuls that this is simply not true in their case because the first they knew about the affair was a long time after it had begun. How could they possibly have 'donated' their partner in any way? The answer is simple: however devious the unfaithfuls, the faithfuls always know an affair has begun. It's just that sometimes they refuse to recognize the signs. Infidelity always shows up in one way or another.

Changes in the quality of the sex life is one common way. Often (surprisingly) the sex actually gets better; sometimes the partner is less interested. Perhaps there is a change in the technique, style or mood of the unfaithful partner in bed. The change can be very obvious or very subtle but, either way, if an affair is going on, it usually shows up in the sex life.

Then there are the absolutely classic signs: husbands working late at the office, wives mysteriously not at home when the husband unexpectedly calls up and so on, right through to tell-tale lipstick on shirts or unfamiliar perfume.

We have found that faithfuls whose partners are unfaithful have actually had to expend far more psychic energy in *not* admitting to the signs than they would have done in acknowledging them. It's hard work to notice something and then to have to fool yourself that you didn't!

In some cases this reluctance to see the writing emblazoned on the wall is only a minor cause of the triangle. But in others it is absolutely critical: had the faithful been less of a Donor he or she would have seen what was happening and prevented it. But Donors feel that there is someone else who has more claim to their lover or else that the third party is invincibly impressive by comparison with them and bound to win, so deep down they want, or expect, the third party to come along and get their lover. So not only do Donors ignore signs of infidelity and fail to put up a fight when the facts are blatantly obvious even to them; in addition, sometimes they actually promote the infidelity by their behaviour.

The triangular Donor

Always faithful, Donors have a problem that can be described like this: they want to give Mummy back to Daddy (if female) or Daddy back to Mummy (if male). The Donor is the flip side of the Snatcher coin: the opposite of snatching from a couple is donating your partner to a third party. Not surprisingly, most Donors are unaware of their motives. But, as in the case of the Snatcher, there is a good deal of subtlety in the way that they make their donation.

The most obvious method is to say, 'Go ahead. I'm broadminded. We have an open relationship, and if you want to sleep with him/her, then fine.' Of course, this is said by types other than the Donor, but what distinguishes Donors is, first, that they don't make as much use of the arrangement as their partner; second, that they take a keen interest in what the partner does with the third party, including sexual details; and, third, that they may actually matchmake for their partner.

This method is less common than the battery of more

implicit techniques. For example, Donors may encourage a friendship with their partner which is obviously going to end up in bed. Afterwards the Donor is furious, but careful examination of the preceding events shows that there were numerous opportunities for protest and that the signals were almost impossible to ignore – except by a Donor, that is. Another common occurrence is a very token resistance: Donors can see that their partner is getting involved with someone else but are prevented by their Donor tendencies from objecting. In such cases they may admire the third party and feel, to some extent, that their partner is right to be getting involved because the third party is a better bet, more attractive or more impressive, than they are. Finally, a less common implicit technique employed by Donors is to drive their partner to infidelity by criticizing the partner's looks or sexual prowess or by running themselves down ('You don't really want someone as stupid/fat/ugly as me') to the point that they manage to sell the idea that they're no good and the partner seeks someone else.

So Donors, whether by implicit or explicit means, actively propagate their partners' affairs out of guilt: they feel that their partners are not rightfully theirs and that any third party with a mind to do so (particularly a Snatcher) should be able to take advantage of the opportunity this presents.

UNFAITHFUL LUST: THE SPLITTER

Personality profile

Dimension: **Lust**
Type: **Splitter**
Position in triangle: **The unfaithful**
Famous examples of this sexual personality type: Deirdre Barlow, Jack Duckworth and Bet Lynch (all in *Coronation Street*), Cecil Parkinson, Henry VIII, President J. F. Kennedy, Dirty Den (*EastEnders*)

General profile

Splitters are dogged by bad luck in long-term sexual relationships. For some strange reason, things always seem to go wrong after a while. Either there's only sex and nothing else, or the relationship starts passionately enough but then desire seems to wane and the sex becomes problematic. But the problem is nothing that a little imagination can't handle. And Splitters have plenty of bright ideas to pep up their sex lives.

Some Splitters find their partner a bit of a turn-off, although they still love them very much. Women Splitters become too tense or just not interested, and men have problems getting aroused. To combat this they do all sorts of exciting things so as to rekindle their desire. They start making love in all manner of different places, or they start dressing up. Some use stimulants like alcohol to get them going; others may even smoke marijuana to relax them. Those with an even more vivid imagination may from time to time pretend that their partner is a favourite movie, pop or other sex symbol, and that can work a treat.

Other Splitters both love and fancy their partner but find their sex life is less than 100 per cent. The men mysteriously lose interest halfway through, or become excited so rapidly that they climax before the woman is ready. Women Splitters may find themselves feeling detached and uninterested during intercourse, or they may feel fed up because their passion comes in brief bursts and the man is unable to respond at the right time. Both are liable to feel very uneasy once the lust has gone; they may find the whole business distasteful, even disgusting.

In fact, all Splitters are prone to find sex a bit dirty, wicked and guilt-inducing at times. It's not surprising that they feel a bit degraded by it. After all, it is a pretty messy business. Their critical feelings may be turned against their partner and express themselves in thoughts such as 'She's so superficial – why do I bother?' or 'He's so insensitive – he just has his way with me and rolls over. No contact, no humanity. He's just an animal.' Or the criticisms may be voiced – 'Why don't you redecorate this place? It's so dowdy,' or 'This place is absolutely filthy. Why don't you get a proper job so we can afford a decent place?' The criticisms come in many forms and may be well deserved, but they're most likely to pop up when sex rears its ugly head. But it's not only after sex that Splitters get like this – if they fancy someone, strangely enough, they may express their feelings through criticism: 'I suppose she's got a nice body, but she's a real bungalow up top,' 'Nice legs, shame about the face,' 'Good-looking, yes, but he's so arrogant and full of himself. He thinks he can have anyone he wants.'

So how do Splitters cope when they get bored by their lover – apart, that is, from by using their imagination? Well, they still love their partner, so sometimes they do what seems the sensible thing – they take another lover and have an affair. It's either that or an end to the relationship, so in a way it's for the good of both of them: sex from the affair, love from the relationship. It's not perfection, but life seldom is.

But then all Splitters, whether attached or not, have lively minds, and sex is on them for a lot of the time. Colleagues at work, acquaintances in their social set, strangers seated across the aisle on the bus, fleeting figures glimpsed briefly in shops – almost anyone, anywhere, may become the object of a Splitter fantasy. The ingenious Splitter tends to invent two types of imagining: the pure, ideal, aloof, untouchable, obscure object of a desire that can never be fulfilled and the sexy, primitive, lustful, available lay who just can't wait to get it. But Splitters can be a real puzzle because if they ever get anywhere near these fantasy people, they become all shy and unable to get their act together. A childlike innocence and blushful modesty overcomes them and, tongue-tied, they retire mumbling from the scene. A bundle of contradictions, the Splitter can become like someone out on a first date at the wink of an eye.

The Splitter has only two ways of seeing members of the opposite sex whom they know well: either as lovers they don't respect or as friends they don't fancy. They see either a body or a person but never both at the same time. And when they fall in love with someone, sooner or later one of two things happens: they begin to love the person but not the body, or they only love the body and not the person. Either the lover becomes as close and predictable as a family member, or all affection is denied and the lover is good for just one thing.

Lustful and blushful, sinful and angelic, caught between fantasy and reality, sex-mad and revolted – that's the Splitter. And why are they called Splitters? Because they split their desire from their affection: they don't love what they fancy, and they don't fancy what they love.

The psychology of the Splitter

Human beings are not like rabbits. They don't come on heat, a period of time in animals when there is a chemical need to have sex as often as possible in order to reproduce. Nor are we like some kind of pressure cooker, with a quantum of sexual energy that must be released regularly or else we'll explode. Not anyone will do – people are attracted only to particular individuals. And, to put it bluntly, if human beings are sexually frustrated, they can always masturbate and at any time in the year.

Human beings don't get frustrated because of an in-built need to have a certain number of orgasms per month. Many people feel sexually frustrated even though they have a perfectly satisfactory sexual relationship with their partner. People start seeking sex with more than one partner for more complex reasons than animal frustration.

When we weigh up the pros and cons of infidelity from the unfaithful's standpoint, it certainly makes more sense for him or her than for the faithful or the third party. None the less it tends to be an agonizing business. Should the faithful be told? If not, how to keep up the deception without getting caught? How to meet both lovers' demands? How to choose which one to stay with if it comes to that? There are so many problems you might wonder if it's worth it.

But there are classic scenarios where it does seem to be: a frustrated spouse who wants a sex life but doesn't want to split up the family, a man whose wife is getting old and who meets a younger woman who wants him, a woman whose husband is a boring workaholic but who can't face all the agony and disruption of separation and divorce. And, of course – very, very rarely in my experience – there is the genuine case of a person who loves two people intensely and cannot bear to give up either.

What all these situations have in common is the presence of splitting on the part of the unfaithful. Generally the unfaithful has a loving, respectful but erotically less inspired relationship with one of the lovers, whereas the relationship with the other is more carnal, based on sex rather than love. This split between desire and affection is present in all of us to some degree because all of us have to learn at a very early age that we must not desire the members of our immediate family, only love them. But for those who had to do this very extremely in childhood familiarity in later life is an automatic turn-off: it reminds them of the childhood situation.

Most of us manage to organize things so that, at the very least, we lust after our partner at times and love him or her at others; if we are lucky, we manage to do both simultaneously. But Splitters are unable to do this. Either they keep their partner at arm's length, or the lust disappears and, although they still love their partner, they find themselves seeking a different partner for sex: the attraction of the new partner lies in his or her unfamiliarity.

Splitters often say that it's certain special characteristics of the third party that turn them on. This is true in the sense that they choose people who present a contrast to their faithful partner. That way there is no danger that they will be reminded of the familiar partner, who may well resemble some aspect of their mother or father or siblings in looks or personality.

The main factor for the Splitter is the fact that the third party is unfamiliar and that he or she is different from the regular partner. This even applies to the older married man/younger woman secretary scenario, a classic situation in which it is widely believed that it is the 'obviously greater' desirability of a woman in her twenties as compared with a middle-aged wife that is crucial. But when the married Splitter leaves his wife to live with his secretary, his desire for her declines rapidly and predictably. Familiarity doesn't breed contempt, but it does put the mockers on the sex life of a Splitter. In such cases it cannot be merely the secretary's youth that inspires the lust.

The triangular Splitter

Splitters are liable to be unfaithful. They are the classic case of the partner for whom desire has dried up in a relationship or who is unaffectionate but full of lust.

Splitters can become unfaithful to their partner for several reasons. The most common cause is a loss of desire for the faithful. Women Splitters become frigid or stop feeling involved during the sex act – they lie back and don't enjoy it. Male Splitters ejaculate prematurely, or have no orgasm, or are actually unable to become erect. At times, both are liable to feel disgusted by the feel of their partner's body, the smell of sex, the partner's desire.

Slightly less common is the Splitter who only desires the partner and otherwise feels hostility, dislike or disgust. Splitters tend to feel rather depraved as well as excited by the 'naughtiness' of their bed-life and afterwards to be critical, even nasty, to their partner.

Splitters are prone to obsession (particularly men) and/or hysteria (particularly women), which can put their partner off. The obsessional Splitter may insist on unreasonable levels of tidiness or cleanliness in the bedroom or kitchen or throughout the house. Hysterical Splitters may make mountains out of molehills and generally behave like a cross between Woody Allen and Adolf Hitler; they make a crisis out of a minor event.

Splitters who no longer desire their faithful partner become frustrated as well as wanting to prove to themselves that they still have a libido and are attractive. They take a lover whom they think of as 'very sexy' and at the same time regard their faithful partner as worthy, lovable and reliable – like an old Labrador. The new lover is not respected or loved and has none of the faithful's characteristics. So unfaithful Splitters come to see all their sexual difficulties as related to the faithful's dull performance in bed, and they believe that this is the crucial factor about the new lover – he/she is just so much more sexy. It saddens them that they don't desire their faithful partners, but the relationship has become like that of brother and sister, and it just can't be helped.

Frustrated unfaithful Splitters will find a willing 'animal sex' third-party lover. They exult in the fact that they just 'do it' together and then the unfaithful goes off home – no strings attached, no complications, no messy love involved. Consequently the Splitter can be cruel and may chuck the lover out after the sex with the words 'I've got to be getting back to my partner now.'

Where Splitters feel only desire and no affection or respect for a faithful partner, the situation is reversed. They criticize and abuse their partner while having wild and abandoned sex with them, and they take a lover whom they respect and love. The sex with the third party in such cases is not the most important thing; rather, it's some special quality that they admire and that they feel the faithful lacks – regardless of whether this is actually true.

THE DONOR–SPLITTER DIAGNOSIS

Your answers to the test on page 31 will reveal that you are either a Donor (D) or a Splitter (S). Check them against the list below to diagnose your sexual personality type. Count the score for each type. The highest score indicates your tendency on the lust dimension.

1.   Yes = S   No = D
2.   Yes = D   No = S

3.	Yes = S	No = D
4.	Yes = D	No = S
5.	Yes = S	No = D
6.	Yes = D	No = S
7.	Yes = S	No = D
8.	Yes = D	No = S
9.	Yes = S	No = D
10.	Yes = D	No = S
11.	Yes = S	No = D
12.	Yes = D	No = S
13.	Yes = D	No = S
14.	Yes = S	No = D
15.	Yes = D	No = S
16.	Yes = S	No = D
17.	Yes = S	No = D
18.	Yes = S	No = D
19.	Yes = D	No = S
20.	Yes = S	No = D

But what if you're neither of these two types? What if you are a third party in a sexual triangle? To complete the picture, what follows is an analysis of why third parties prey on couples.

THIRD-PARTY LUST: THE SNATCHER

Personality profile

Dimension: **Lust**

Type: **The Snatcher**

Position in triangle: **The third party**

Famous examples of this sexual personality type: Mike Baldwin (*Coronation Street*), Catherine Wentworth (who tried to kill J.R. and snatch Bobby Ewing in *Dallas*), Sarah Keays, Mags (who snatched Dirty Den from Angie in *EastEnders*), Pat (who tried to snatch Dirty Den)

General profile

Snatchers have a tendency to get involved with people who are already going out with someone else. Anybody can be a Snatcher, whether introvert or extrovert, aggressive or passive, cheerful or miserable. The wonderful thing about Snatchers is that they can change their personality like a chameleon when they're doing what they like doing best – snatching! They find it intolerable to see people they love going stale in ordinary, mundane, 'We're going steady' or 'We're happily married' relationships. They add spice to the lives of these unhappy couples by trying to snatch one of them. They've got a lot to give, Snatchers, and they can't bear to see a desirable and attractive person wasting away in a mediocre, destructive relationship. They jump in, hoping to prevent a lifetime's misery and to supplant it with the love they've got to give.

Some Snatchers never actually succeed in parting shaky couples. However, they have a lot of fun in trying to do so. Deep down they feel a sympathy for the faithful, and their compassion gets the better of them. Some know that you have to be cruel to be kind, and they go the whole hog, successfully breaking up the couple and liberating the person they love from someone who was absolutely no good for him or her. Others seduce the object of their desire and, for a short period, are intensely satisfied. But what marks these Snatchers out is that once they have achieved their goal the desire evaporates and the affair ends. Such Snatchers notice this pattern, but they try not to let it worry them.

You will often find Snatchers on the edge of other people's relationships. For instance, they may go on holiday, alone, with friends who are a couple. During the holiday they will be busy snatching. It may be done obviously or secretly, but you can be sure that they're hard at work: 'He always seemed to end up in the kitchen with me, talking about this and that, nonsense, really. But those times on our own together were when I first realized I felt for him.' 'She started sunbathing topless on the deck with me and Angie. We pretended to be so cool about it, but she was really turning me on, and she knew it.' The Snatcher's early moves. For some Snatchers all this manoeuvring and scheming is the best bit – the thrill of the chase. It's hard work saving someone you love from a miserable relationship, but it can be fun too. There is a certain enjoyment to be had from agonizing over what to do and whether it is right. It's romantic. It makes you feel alive.

Some Snatchers end up stealing their best friend's girl or their best friend's man. They know their best friends well and can tell if their lovers are right for them or not. Sometimes, it has to be admitted, they are more suited to the Snatcher: 'After all, how was she to know that she would love me more? It was only through meeting my best friend that she got to know me at all. Such a shame we didn't meet first.' All Snatchers have a tendency to feel that they are better suited than the faithful and that the unfaithful will be happier with them.

The ever-adaptable Snatcher may be forced to point out to the lover some of the best friend's shortcomings in the attempt to help the unfaithful to admit the truth. The Snatcher may be devious, but he or she is falling in love, and nothing else matters.

Snatchers suffer pangs of guilt afterwards, even though they are only acting out of the best of motives. They feel it is their duty, as honest and decent people, to inform the faithful party of precisely what has occurred. It is crucial that no detail be spared, they feel, since there is a danger that unexplained aspects of the affair may play on the unhappy person's mind: 'It's better that you hear it from the horse's mouth, and I swear I shan't hold anything back from you. This time I want to be totally honest.'

Inexplicably, all Snatchers are subject to depression at some point after the affair has taken place. Some may even go to the extraordinary length of trying to make amends to the injured party. The Florence Nightingales of relationships, Snatchers seek to heal the injury and to nurse the pain in others, yet they themselves suffer deeply. For all their efforts this is their reward. 'I never really wanted to hurt his wife. She sounded such a good person, really nice. But I was being hurt too, you know. She was having him for the whole weekend. But I did want to make amends . . .'

Another curious feature of snatching is the way that Snatchers' sexual desire tends to decrease once they have 'saved' the unfaithful. It's as if they have a built-in mechanism which ensures that their caring activities are never restricted to just one person – once the desire has gone the affair ends, and they seek a new partner. In fact, whether married or not, Snatchers always feel the need to carry out their role and, sadly but inevitably, this means that they rarely have long-term relationships.

Not surprisingly, Snatchers have a tricky time when they fall in love. They may drink or smoke heavily, gamble or take unnecessary risks when driving, or they may work compulsively or suffer from psychosomatic symptoms like headaches and an unsettled stomach. It's a hard life for Snatchers, always living in the shadow of another person. Nobody thanks them for their efforts on behalf of others: 'What did I do last night when you were with your husband? I got pissed, that's what I did. It's unbearable being away from you for more than a moment.'

However, their sex life is very exciting, reaching the peaks at times, all-time lows at others. Covert meetings with unfaithfuls will sometimes be the most thrilling and gratifying of orgasmic releases, unfettered lust and love combined in completely fresh ways. Yet at other times there is a puzzling constraint, a lack of that extra something so vital for real gratification. 'It's just mechanical. Yet we love each other. What's missing? What can we do?' At other times still, encounters are acutely uncomfortable, awkward even – as though there were someone else watching. The Snatcher sighs. The job is done, and it's time to call it a day.

Breaker and maker, devious and honest, a lone liberator, in demand and at risk of being dumped – that's the Snatcher. Some of your best friends are Snatchers. They may lurk on the edge of your relationship with your partner, but they know the truth behind your joint façade. Watch out! There's a Snatcher about!

The psychology of the Snatcher

Why do Snatchers prey on couples? Jealousy. Feeling left out. Having to arrange your love life around someone else's schedule. Anxiety about whether it'll last. Yes, that's the lot of the third party. In return, they get a part-time lover and no strings attached, but you've got to wonder: why do they bother?

Sigmund Freud offered a convincing answer to this question, which cases have confirmed again and again. In a paper entitled 'Contributions to the Psychology of Love' he stated that there were three 'conditions' which anyone (but particularly men) who is motivated by an urge to snatch requires:

1. A faithful who will be injured by the affair. In other words, hurting the faithful by winning the competition for the unfaithful is crucial. Single lovers are therefore not as interesting to the true Snatcher.

2. The feeling that the unfaithful is in some way both very special and very sexy. The unfaithful is an ideal, and their joint love is felt to be inevitable and all consuming.

3. The feeling that the unfaithful needs to be rescued from some dire situation, probably the relationship with the faithful (but not necessarily – I have come across cases in which the Snatcher felt the unfaithful deserved better housing, a more opulent lifestyle, a better social life and so forth).

Now, most third parties will deny that these motives apply to them. In particular, they will deny that the faithful has anything to do with it and will insist that it is purely the mutual feeling between them and the unfaithful that counts. They may never even have met the faithful or know anything about him or her. Nevertheless, closer inspection invariably reveals that all three of the conditions listed above play some part, however small, in any third party's motivation. Just as the Donor manages not to recognize signs of the affair, so the Snatcher struggles to ignore the fact that the relationship is only one of two that the unfaithful is enjoying simultaneously. The 'splitting' of unfaithful partners naturally aids this process, of course: they do not want to be reminded of their relationship with the faithful when with the third party. So both conspire to ignore the other relationship. But in reality the adulterous affair always exists to some extent only because there is an original couple.

The proof of this is to be found in the cases of Snatchers who are so successful that the unfaithful actually comes to live with them. Just as an unfaithful Splitter's desire rapidly wanes in such circumstances, so it is with the Snatcher. Having achieved the goal of stealing Mummy from Daddy (or vice versa), the attraction of the unfaithful wanes for Snatchers – they become either Donors or unfaithful Splitters themselves until they get rid of the unfaithful!

Of course, what we have been saying applies to third parties who have a Snatcher sexual personality type. When snatching is only a tendency, it can be only a marginal motive for the affair. But as a motive within the lust dimension it is important and needs to be looked at carefully before it can be discarded as less than central.

Of course, people sometimes fall in love with attached or married individuals, and the fact of the existence of a faithful is only a very minor factor. But it's always there. If you're a third party, try to examine exactly what you saw in the unfaithful right from the start. If you're honest, you'll be able to remember when you first found out that he or she was already spoken for. How did you feel? If you didn't know, then why not? It's very strange not to find out something like that before you sleep with someone. Did he or she lie? Are you sure you weren't rather easy to take in? Take a long, hard look at the situation before you reject totally the idea that snatching has at some stage played a part in your attraction to your stolen partner.

If you're not a third party but one of a triangle, then it's important to establish to what extent snatching has played a part. If you're an unfaithful, don't be vain. Consider seriously the proposition that the possibility of parting you from the faithful might have been one of your attractions. If you're the faithful, it shouldn't be hard for you to feel you've been the victim of a snatch, so be careful not to overestimate it! You may have had a role in it. And if you're just a member of a couple, take a good look at the Snatcher profile – if one of you becomes unfaithful, then you can be sure that snatching will have played a part. Now's your chance, before it's too late, to form a picture of the type of person who will be trying to lure one of you away.

The triangular Snatcher

By definition Snatchers are always the third party in a triangle. What drives them on can be described as follows: the urge to steal Mummy from Daddy (if male) or Daddy from Mummy (if female). Snatchers hang about on the edge of other couples, and when the moment comes they strike with the deft touch and good timing of a cat. Their sexual relationships do not last long, and they may have a history of sleeping with other people's recent ex-partners as well as the current ones (they like consoling a person who is on the rebound). However, once Snatchers have won the unfaithful from the faithful, they lose interest rapidly. The sex goes off, and they may have a bout of depression.

Snatchers are highly adaptable when in pursuit of their prey. They take careful stock of what the unfaithful is lacking and work hard at providing it or at demonstrating that they could do so. Their object is to show how much better a partner they could be. But if subtlety is required, they will sense it. For example, they won't necessarily criticize the faithful in front of the unfaithful if they realize that he or she is keen to retain a positive image of the partner. On the other hand, if the unfaithful is angry with the faithful, they'll join in tactfully in a character assassination: 'Yes, I see what you mean. I suppose, when you put it like that, he/she always has been a bit of a liar/a bit of a bully/rather selfish,' and so forth, perhaps drawing attention, in the process, to a failing that the unfaithful had not previously noticed. (But this must be done with care because there is a risk of provoking a rush to the defence of the faithful if the unfaithful does not agree.)

Overall, Snatchers usually initiate triangles. Of course, an unfaithful partner who is strongly motivated to have an affair may get a pleasant surprise – someone who is asking to be snatched.

3 THE INSECURITY DIMENSION

Before I explain how insecurity works in couples, it's time to do the second diagnostic test to find out where you are on the insecurity dimension. *It's essential that you do the test before reading what follows.*

To diagnose your personality type, take a clean sheet of paper and write the numbers 1–20 down the left-hand side. To each question answer 'yes' or 'no'.

1. You become highly dependent on your lovers and fear they might abandon you at any time, abruptly.
2. You can be a problem to your friends when drunk.
3. You are highly apologetic if late for appointments.
4. You are passionate, short-tempered and constantly amazed by the stupidity of others.
5. You worry like mad that something awful has happened to a partner if he or she is late.
6. You feel highly critical of others, and you imagine your partner will reject you by having affairs.
7. You drag out partings as long as possible.
8. You are sometimes highly self-critical, pouring scorn on yourself and unable to feel positive about anything.
9. You long for relationships to continue after they are over.
10. You have highly emotional bust-ups when you feel rejected and betrayed. You are prone to fantasies of revenge and may make real attempts to get back at the partner.
11. You visit places, listen to music or treasure objects that remind you of a lost loved one long after he or she has gone.

12. Your sense of humour can be cruel, at times even vicious.
13. You imagine you've seen lost loved ones in the street, on buses, on escalators or in other public places and can hardly believe it wasn't really them.
14. You get very annoyed if someone turns up late for a date.
15. You have to feel very secure and loved by your partner before you desire them.
16. You expect others to understand that if you're late for a date, it's probably for a good reason, and you get annoyed if they make a fuss about it.
17. You don't like long-drawn-out goodbyes and sometimes forget to say goodbye properly.
18. You are sympathetic and supportive when friends have anxieties and emotional problems, and they feel you to be an understanding person.
19. When things go wrong, you carry on as if nothing has happened and believe in keeping a stiff upper lip.
20. You like to be active and quite aggressive during sex.

Before finding out your score and making your diagnosis (see pages 71–2), you must read the following introduction to the insecurity dimension and the profiles of the two types of insecure person.

Insecure? Who can honestly say they never are? No one can. But people vary. Some are insecure only when the chips are down; others worry nearly all the time. Whichever type you are, there are two basic anxieties that afflict people in relationships: the fear of being rejected and the fear of being abandoned. So when we say 'insecure', we're not so much talking about the questions 'Am I OK?', 'Do I look good?' 'Am I clever?', 'Am I up to scratch?' Rather, we are considering the questions 'Will my lover respond to me?', 'Will he or she be there when I need love?' The insecurity dimension is all about fears concerning the responsiveness and the presence or absence of partners.

In childhood we all have to depend on our parents. Parents vary in how dependable they are, how reliably they meet our need for love, comfort and food when they're around and how reliable they are about being there at all (whether or not they leave us unpredictably with strangers, for example). How dependable our parents were during our childhood affects our later love attachments. If they were very unreliable, in later life we expect lovers to be unreliable too. The more unreliable they were, the greater our insecurity in relationships.

Since everybody is insecure at times, the extremes on this dimension are two distinct styles of expressing insecurity.

At one extreme is the type who expects to be rejected because that is what happened in childhood. Being rejected makes you despondent, but it also makes you angry with the person who has rejected you. This is expressed by your own rejection of others: the boot is now on the other foot. This type of person is angry and rejecting because he or she expects rejection in relationships. The name of this type is the Bully.

People at the other end of the insecurity scale expect to be abandoned rather than rejected. They are anxious that a partner will disappear without warning, and they are expecting this to happen at any time. Rather than getting angry, they try to find ways of ensuring that they aren't abandoned – getting angry is hardly the best way. Instead they plead with partners not to go; they try to find out where their lover will be during the day, not because they fear infidelity but because they want to be sure they can get hold of them in an emergency. In the past their parents weren't there at such times, and they don't want this to happen again – in fact, they'll go to almost any length to avoid it. The name of this type is the Clinger.

Some people are insecure most of the time – the fear of rejection or abandonment is never far from their mind, regardless of whether there is a real danger of its happening. Others become insecure only when there is a real reason to worry. At such times even the most secure of us begins to expect rejection or abandonment and to become bullying or clinging. Even at moments when there is little to fear, the risk stimulates irrational fears, dredging up long-forgotten childhood incidents in which we felt abandoned or rejected by those we loved.

Just as people vary in how insecure they are overall, so they vary in the degree to which they tend to be exclusively Bullies or Clingers when they are insecure. Everyone tends to incline one way more than the other, but equally everyone is both sometimes: on occasions everybody bullies and everybody clings. So in deciding who's who on this dimension, you must bear in mind that people are always to some extent both, but don't let this fact confuse you. Taken in the round, everyone tends more towards one type.

Insecurity is a major cause of problems in relationships when one partner (or both) has a Bully or a Clinger sexual personality type. If either partner is continually expecting things to go wrong, they may actually do so. Both Bullies and Clingers can drive their partner into the arms of another, or else they embark on affairs themselves to allay their imaginary fears. In particular, their expectation that they will be rejected or abandoned can be so insistent that it actually leads their partner to leave them!

People with a Bully or Clinger sexual personality type have a tendency to end up with their opposite: Bullies find a Clinger easy to push around because Clingers will do anything to hang on to their lover and because the clinging is an antidote to the Bully's feeling of being rejected. For their part, Clingers feel safe if they have someone who runs their life for them even if they are terrified by the angry outbursts. So Bully–Clinger relationships are quite common.

Bully–Bully or Clinger–Clinger relationships are less common, for obvious reasons. Two Bullies together often have the kind of row which no couple can stand for long, and sooner or later one leaves the other – often for a third party – as an act of revenge for some imagined slight. Two Clingers, on the other hand, make a couple that, although shot full of anxiety, is quite stable. Each is more concerned with the risk of abandonment than with seeking lovers, and they tend to cling to each other like glue.

So who's who on the insecurity dimension for you and your lover(s)? Read the general profiles and the triangular tendencies of the Bully and Clinger, then use the test to double-check your first impressions. Remember, everyone is a Bully or a Clinger to some extent, even if it's only when the sparks are flying. Try to keep an open mind as to whether or not one of them is your sexual personality type. Remember too that it's easy to write other people off as Bullies or Clingers, but it's not so easy to admit to insecurity yourself.

THE BULLY

Personality profile

Dimension: **Insecurity**

Type: **Bully**

Position in triangle: **Any**

Famous examples of this sexual personality type: Ivy Tilsley and Percy Sugden (*Coronation Street*), J. R. Ewing and Cliff Barnes (*Dallas*), John McEnroe, George Best, Adolf Hitler, John Lennon, Basil Fawlty (*Fawlty Towers*), Margaret Thatcher, Arthur Scargill, Attila the Hun, Napoleon, Lady Macbeth, Mary the Punk and Nick Cotton (*EastEnders*)

General profile

Bullies are angry young men or women, whatever their age. They feel very passionate about a lot of things and never cease to be amazed at people's stupidity concerning these important issues. Their patience is constantly being tried. They're liable to express their frustration by losing their temper (and do Bullies have a temper!) or in bouts of depression. Can you blame them? They're surrounded by people who don't understand that half-measures and compromise only make matters worse. They know what is required, and they're damned if they'll put up with an incompetent, botched job: 'It's no good. I'm not having this wall papered over when it's so uneven. Either we replaster it ourselves now or we get in professionals. No, no, that's enough! OK, we get in the decorators and bugger the cost.'

Bullies hate inefficiency when there's no need. If you turn up late for a date and have missed the start of the film, not surprisingly they get annoyed: 'I'm really not sure if I want to see it now. I did when I got here, but I'm not sure now. I mean, you could be a bit more considerate – you're always late. Get yourself better organized.' And they may not have calmed down by the time the film's over. It's not that they bear a grudge; it's just that they find it hard to forget when they've been mucked about.

When Bullies turn up late, on the other hand, there's always a very good reason, and they expect you to understand that. They always try their best, and if you don't know that, then you can't really love your Bully. And don't try the 'You're such a hypocrite' argument with them because it really would be the last straw: 'The bus was LATE, L-A-T-E, LATE. If you can't see a difference between a LATE BUS and just being late for any old reason, then you're stupider than I thought.' Bullies are expert at putting their case.

They have no time for social niceties. When meeting them, don't expect a superficial, conventional 'Hello' – smile – 'Hello' – smile – look in the eye – 'How are you?' routine. More likely, they'll be too wrapped up in something to notice you or else so pleased to see you that you can't get a word in edgeways. And the same goes for partings. No 'Goodbye – how nice to have seen you' or 'See you soon – 'bye' from Bullies. They're more impulsive than that. They may suddenly start acting as if you're not there just before they go, or they're liable to nip off without so much as a 'by your leave'.

You wonder where they've got to, but they're miles away already with a bee in their bonnet about something new.

And when Bullies get an idea in their head it can become all-engrossing. They can be fascinating people to listen to as they explain their system of thought; be it Marxism or Fascism, feminism or chauvinism, religion or science, they'll argue vehemently for its purest form. They know their stuff, and they love to argue.

Sometimes people mistake reasoned argument for rowing, and that can lead to misunderstandings with friends: 'I hate it when he gets like this. Why does he have to turn it into a row? He can't see the other point of view.' But Bullies *can* see the other person's point. That's precisely why they're arguing: 'That's why I'm explaining it again, so you can properly understand the point. You wouldn't be saying what you're saying if you really understood what *I'm* saying.' You may think they're treating you as stupid at this point, and some Bullies do get criticized as tactless and inconsiderate. And this *can* appear to be the case, especially when they insist on joining in with whatever's going on and spoiling it by what others see as 'uncooperative', 'domineering', 'egotistical' behaviour. But that's not the way it is. The Bully's natural vigour and passion are once more being misunderstood.

Bullies know how valuable they are to have around when the chips are down. They'll sort out all your problems and see you right through that sticky patch with absolute commitment: 'Right. You've got to move out of that house – that's the first thing. And you've got to do it now. Yes, now. You can sleep at my place. I'll take the sofa, and you can get some proper sleep. Then I'll . . .' But people never thank Bullies for helping them. They just exploit their help and then turn round and kick them in the face: 'She just totally took me over. I couldn't even make a cup of tea or go out to the shops. Mind you, she was a tower of strength in a time of need.' And Bullies feel they can be helpful to everyone. They're born leaders who'll cut through all the nonsense. A few have been great politicians, statesmen, world leaders, people who through the sheer force of their personalities have changed the course of history.

But self-doubt gets in the way if you're that kind of person, so Bullies have to be resolute, domineering even; they know that other people are highly unreliable and will always take the soft option if given the chance. They know the very real risk of betrayal and rejection in every relationship, whether professional or personal, so they're shrewd enough to get in first if necessary. The Bully will really have to trust you before he or she will give you the chance to inflict hurt or damage – no Bully will let you see his or her soft and vulnerable side until then. In relationships the worldly-wise Bully senses any sign of infidelity almost before you know you are having any such thoughts. And if Bullies are unfaithful, there won't be any hypocritical sympathy because 'I know you were planning on chucking me anyhow. I'm only doing what you've probably done countless times.' You can't fool the uncompromising Bully.

Small wonder, then, given such a stormy love life, that there are spectacular bust-ups, often leading to divorce. Betrayed and rejected, the Bully becomes a raging torrent of anger that no one and nothing can stem. It's the stuff of films, the big screen – shouting matches, fights, bitter recriminations. The Bully arrives unexpectedly in the middle of the night, smashing crockery, hurling furniture aside and making irreversible pledges such as 'I never want to see you again, ever, for the rest of my life,' and saying the most hurtful things imaginable: 'You want to hear the truth? You're fat, ugly, and whenever I had sex with you I was thinking of someone else.' Like most people, Bullies may resort to drink at such times, and they can be a problem to their friends when under the influence; they may have to be helped home or dragged away from fights or quietened down in heated arguments. They're really colourful characters, Bullies.

But they have to suffer for their forcefulness and directness. At times they get very depressed; ever the perfectionist, they become highly self-critical. They will pour scorn on themselves, feeling worse than useless. Exacting in their standards for others, they are no less rigorous with themselves, and it is this very quality that makes them so effective as charismatic leaders. But not all Bullies achieve their potential. Some become very downcast as the years go by. They get bitter and resentful in love and at work. They blame other people for their own mistakes, feel that they have been hard done by and misunderstood. They say, 'They always twist round what you say and use it against you. People are just plain evil. Look at the way they ganged up against me. They were out to get me from the start.' Sadly, Bullies can never tell you who 'they' are.

When loved ones die they will often find it hard to acknowledge their feelings, pretending the death has not occurred and carrying on as if nothing has happened, refusing to talk about it. They lock it all up deep inside. At such times they may be unusually accident-prone. They may be involved in a potentially lethal car crash or may accidentally cut themselves while carving. (Bullies often have bad luck.) But it's not all bad news for Bullies. They'll often enjoy a good joke, and they've got a keen, sarcastic sense of humour.

At work, Bullies' ability and ambition rarely match their actual achievements. They have a vision and dynamism that few bosses and colleagues can fully appreciate, and the ensuing rows do not help promotion prospects. Small-minded people may say, 'But it's going to cost far too much money and take far too long if we do things your way.' The Bully replies, 'No, it won't. Can't you use your imagination, for God's sake? *I*'m not frightened of hard work even if you are. It's simple, we just halve the lunch hour or cut the coffee break to five minutes. I'm going to work right through. I don't need a break, so why should they?'

In bed all Bullies blow hot and cold. They can be very active or vulnerable and in need of loving reassurance. It's particularly important that they find the right partner; only certain people suit them because they know what turns Bullies on (and Bullies have very well-defined ideas about love-making). Being active and forceful, female Bullies may find it hard to persuade men to overcome the conditioning which prevents them from accepting a woman who leads the way, whereas the way that women have been taught to behave suits male Bullies better – they like to give their partner a really good time, even if it does get a bit rough on occasions!

Charismatic yet depressed, hurt yet angry, convinced and convincing – that's the Bully. Bullies are pillars of strength yet, deep down, they're lost and alone and desperately in need of love.

The triangular Bully

Bullies are anxious in relationships and make shaky partners. As faithfuls they are particularly prone to feeling abused and betrayed and to creating an unfaithful partner out of a lover. Bullies blame the other participants if they get into a triangle, and they often end up alienating all concerned.

The faithful Bully

There are a great number of ways in which Bullies may alienate their lovers. They throw temper-tantrums about seemingly tiny issues and start rows over nothing. They are liable to harangue a lover and are unable to admit it when they're wrong. They get paranoid about whether their partner's faithful when there's nothing to fear, but they go on about it so much that, in the end, they have every reason to worry. They reject attempts to patch up quarrels, giving rebuffs where others might bury the hatchet. They bear grudges. They get depressed in bouts and are inconsolable. They run hot and cold in bed – great sometimes, a wash-out at others. They try to help their partner run his or her life but are too interfering in the end. Small wonder, then, that Bullies are so often the victims of infidelity.

The unfaithful Bully

To Bullies revenge is sweet, and an act of infidelity may be the chosen method. Unfortunately, Bullies are all too likely to retaliate against someone who has never done them any harm in the first place, but so sure are they of being spurned and rejected that they cannot be made to see this. Sometimes they are so insecure about their partner's love that they have an affair just to avoid an inevitable rejection – they put the rejecting boot on the other foot. At other times they may feel that their partner is too domineering and doesn't appreciate them. A suitably admiring third party will find this Bully easy meat.

The third-party Bully

Bullies may be attracted by lack of commitment and the ambiguity of being in this role. They get all the fun without the fear of being cheated on. They're particularly likely to succeed where there is a troubled, weakly bonded couple that they can muscle in on. In such cases Bullies may put on a display of charismatic impressiveness, and it wins the day. However, the main problem a Bully faces as a third party is finding an unfaithful who suits him or her – Bullies must avoid losing their tempers and tone down their less pleasant side if they are to succeed.

THE CLINGER

Personality profile

Dimension: **Insecurity**
Type: **Clinger**
Position in triangle: **Any**
Famous examples of this sexual personality type: Mavis Riley and Stan Ogden (*Coronation Street*), Sue-Ellen Ewing (*Dallas*), Macbeth, Bryan Ferry, the Hunchback of Notre Dame, Angie Watts (*EastEnders*)

General profile

Clingers are considerate, sometimes to the point of fussiness. They'll take great care to establish exactly where and when to meet their lover: 'Outside the cinema? Or inside the foyer? About seven-ish? Do you mean seven or five past?'. They need to avoid any blunders. Turn up late for a Clinger, and they may have made anxious phone calls to find out where you've got to. But they're not angry; they're just worried about what might have happened to you. After all, you might have had an accident. Anyway, you're here now so all's well. What a relief!

If the Clinger is late, there'll be plenty of apologies and perhaps a long story explaining why. 'And then I realized I'd forgotten my keys, and it was too late to ring you and . . .' They're very relieved that you waited, though, because 'I was *sure* you wouldn't still be there.' That's the basic point about Clingers: they always *expect* to be abandoned.

When you meet Clingers, their reaction is a bit confusing. Deep down they're really happy to see you, but they act shy, offhand or a bit distant. When you get to know and love your Clinger this ceases to worry you, and you sometimes have to interpret their reactions to mutual friends: 'He is really happy to see you, you know – he just doesn't show it.' Saying goodbye to Clingers is no simpler. There's always another thing the Clinger has just remembered: 'Oh, by the way, the party's next Friday week, I think – or is it Saturday? I'll tell you tomorrow. OK, then, well, see you. Oh, have you finished with that book? Did you enjoy it?' Always allow an extra half hour when saying goodbye to a Clinger! And they're just as bad when *you*'re leaving. 'Oh, do have another coffee – it's not that late. Your coat's behind the door. You ought to get the lining mended. It's a nice coat. Isn't it the one that . . . Oh, well, see you then. 'Bye. Is this your scarf?' A relationship with a Clinger is a tale of comings and goings, of closeness creating distance, of approach and avoidance.

Some Clingers find socializing very difficult. They're shy; strangers make them nervous and they have difficulty in putting on a good social act. They tend to have only a few very close friends upon whom they depend. Lesser friends tend to exploit them by using their shoulder to cry on. These

Clingers are a dumping ground for other people's problems. Sometimes they complain about it, but when someone needs help somehow these Clingers are always there – they like to feel wanted, and they like helping people. In their sexual relationships these Clingers get intensely involved and like to make major commitments. When things go wrong, they have trouble accepting it. They'll tend to ring up the lost lover, to create hysterical scenes, even to turn up at their homes at all hours of the day and night. In fact, they cling like mad. They always feel they've been chucked. They get let down and suffer as a result.

The socializing of other Clingers seems superficially to be rather different. They put on a bright front, but this highly competent social presence is a mask hiding insecurities. 'It seems like I've got loads of friends but really I've got very few,' they might write in their diary. For them loneliness is a crowded room. They keep up an independent image; they travel light; they don't want to hear about most people's problems because 'I don't want to get involved.' Not surprisingly, these Clingers avoid intense commitments in their sexual relationships, tending to live alone for as long as possible. In most cases they succumb eventually to their clinging tendencies and become heavily committed or, as they would put it, they 'accept more responsibilities'. But then, of course, they are vulnerable to being let down and all the suffering that entails.

Both kinds of Clinger are prone to broken love affairs, and they have as much difficulty coping with bereavement as with bust-ups in their love life. They can't accept that the lost person has gone. They are liable to imagine they have seen them in the street or on a bus. They will visit places linked with them and attach enormous significance to sentimental objects that they once shared – perhaps a shell from a beach or a faded photograph. Often they will find themselves seeking the company of people that remind them of the absent loved one.

Clingers are liable to be highly self-critical and often feel apathetic and fed up, though they may hide their feelings by putting on a brave face. They realize that basically they're alone, and it gets them down – there's always a sense of abandonment. Sometimes they feel so abandoned that they may contemplate, or in extreme circumstances attempt, suicide.

The Clinger is a nervy type. House moves, job changes, accidents, travelling – any major change in their life makes them very anxious. This is often expressed in particular fears about health, about staying in, about going out: 'I must see the doctor about this rash. I'm sure it's something serious, but it's such a long way on the bus and I really hate going on the Underground.'

They don't like uncertainty at work either. On the whole, Clingers want jobs where they know where they are. They can get quite panicky when there's a flap on in the office. If they work outside the home, they want a stable, secure environment. Many prefer to be their own bosses so that things are under their control.

Lying in bed with a lover, Clingers need to feel really loved if they're to relax and enjoy sex. They may say, 'Let's cuddle for a while. I just want to feel close for a bit.' They tend not to initiate sexual activity and will join in only when they feel they are really wanted. They hate feeling that desire is one-sided. During intercourse itself they are liable to have phases when they don't feel turned on, but that's nothing that a few loving words can't handle. Clingers like to feel loved. So with an unresponsive lover they'll blow hot and cold and seem distant at times, demanding at others. This can make sex a frustrating business for them and their partners.

Hit-and-miss, coming and going, hot and cold, intense and distant – that's the Clinger. Clingers often feel abandoned, and they need to be loved.

The triangular Clinger

Clingers tend to be faithful. They will go to great lengths to hang on to their partners and will put up with a lot to keep a relationship intact. They rarely initiate affairs as third parties but are relatively easy to persuade by a determined unfaithful. They are rarely unfaithfuls themselves: Clingers tend to cling even more if things aren't going well in a relationship; infidelity is rarely their chosen method of solving the problem.

The faithful Clinger

Like the faithful Bully, the Clinger often causes his or her partner to take a lover because of an insecure pattern of relating. Clingers may cling so hard that the relationship becomes suffocating or boring. They may have phobias about being alone or separated from their partner and may pester him or her on the phone at work. They may make endless demands and try to get their partner to run their life for them, to get them to become like a mother with a child. However, they can be puzzling because often when their partner responds and tries to meet their demands, they are distant and ungrateful. The fear of being abandoned (as opposed to spurned, rejected) is never far from Clingers' minds. This fear can be so pronounced that it actually causes the partner to abandon them.

Clingers run hot and cold about sex. They can be very frustrating when all they want is to be coddled and cuddled – they curl up with a partner who then gets sexually aroused, only to be rebuffed because the Clinger wants comfort, not sex, at such times. Clingers' periodic bouts of depression can also be a turn-off. So the Clinger is prone to being a faithful victim of infidelity of their own making.

The unfaithful Clinger

Because the Clinger's reaction to problems in a relationship is to try to get closer, physically and emotionally, to their partner, he or she rarely embarks on affairs as an attempt to solve the problems. 'Revenge sex' with a third party is extremely rare, for example. Only when a desperate need to be close to somebody has arisen, and the faithful is not meeting this need, will Clingers seek a substitute. And this makes Clingers even more anxious – a dread of the faithful finding out and abandoning them altogether will dominate them for days after the act of infidelity. So, on the rare occasions when it happens, the Clinger's fling is probably on impulse and in the arms of someone who is offering comfort and love or who insists that he or she can provide it to the point that the Clinger can't resist the temporary feeling of security it will bring.

The third-party Clinger

A dominating and persuasive person can cajole a Clinger into bed with persistence and good timing. If he or she plays on the Clinger's insecurity skilfully enough, it shouldn't be too hard. However, would-be unfaithfuls must bear in mind that third-party Clingers will be frightened of being abandoned immediately the sex is over, and there may be a fear of reprisals from the faithful partner. So they must be con- vinced, first, that it is not only their body that the unfaithful is after and, second, that the faithful won't mind (saying 'He/she will never find out' may not be enough) before they'll agree.

Clingers very rarely initiate affairs except in so far as they may hang around on the edge of a couple and attach them- selves to the potentially unfaithful – an attachment that may turn into sex if the unfaithful plays the right cards (e.g. by bucking up the Clinger's self-esteem with flattery) or, when the Clinger's friend is the faithful, by showing that the unfaithful likes him or her too.

THE BULLY–CLINGER DIAGNOSIS

Your answers to the test on page 56 will reveal that you are either a Bully (B) or a Clinger (C). Check them against the list below to diagnose your sexual personality type. Count up the scores for each type. The highest score indicates your tendency on the insecurity dimension.

1.	Yes = C	No = B
2.	Yes = B	No = C
3.	Yes = C	No = B
4.	Yes = B	No = C
5.	Yes = C	No = B
6.	Yes = B	No = C
7.	Yes = C	No = B
8.	Yes = B	No = C
9.	Yes = C	No = B
10.	Yes = B	No = C
11.	Yes = C	No = B
12.	Yes = B	No = C
13.	Yes = C	No = B
14.	Yes = B	No = C
15.	Yes = C	No= B
16.	Yes = B	No= C
17.	Yes = B	No = C
18.	Yes = C	No = B
19.	Yes = B	No = C
20.	Yes = B	No = C

4 THE DOMINANCE DIMENSION

Before I explain how dominance works in couples, do the third diagnostic test to find out where you are on the Dominance dimension. *Remember, it's essential that you do the test before reading what follows.*

There are two different tests, one for each sex.

DIAGNOSTIC TEST FOR WOMEN

To diagnose your personality type, take a clean sheet of paper and write the numbers 1–20 down the left-hand side. To each question answer 'yes' or 'no'.

1. You feel you are resisting the traditional role of women.
2. It is far more important to you to belong to the most popular social set in your world than to succeed at work.
3. You feel that you will always *have* to have a boyfriend or husband.
4. You prefer Jackie Collins-type novels to the Barbara Cartland type of romance.
5. You like your man to be dependent on you.
6. In your early twenties you often say (or said) you can't imagine getting married and probably won't have children.
7. You feel that in your life work will always take second place to marriage and children.
8. You are often competitive and openly assertive towards men.
9. You believe that we are all bisexual.
10. You're embarrassed to react emotionally, but you were openly moved by Prince Charles's and Lady Di's wedding ceremony, for example.

11. You expect to go back to work if you do have children.
12. Shopping is a favourite pastime, and you prefer unambiguously feminine clothes for every occasion.
13. You accept that domestic work, like cooking and cleaning, is primarily the woman's responsibility.
14. You think there's nothing wrong with old-fasioned chivalry in a man – for example, offering to pay for a meal or giving up a seat on public transport.
15. You have a constant conflict between being gentle and caring and getting what you want, and you fight the urge to be taken care of by a man, financially or otherwise.
16. To you sex is really a physical thing, not a romantic and dreamy experience.
17. You like the man to do most of the work in bed.
18. You consider there is nothing wrong in opting to be a single parent.
19. You are very concerned that you give pleasure to your man in bed.
20. You often like to be on top during intercourse.

DIAGNOSTIC TEST FOR MEN

To diagnose your personality type, take a clean sheet of paper and write the numbers 1–20 down the left-hand side. To each question answer 'yes' or 'no'.

1. You have a tough, masculine personality.
2. You expect to pay if you take a woman out for the evening, even if she doesn't expect you to.
3. You prefer women who don't try to compete with you.
4. You believe that we are all bisexual.
5. You enjoy competitive sports, either playing or watching.
6. You really enjoy a lively night out with the lads – or you used to.
7. Your dress and basic habits are fairly typical for a person of your background.

8. You tend to fit in with whatever group you're in, at work or play, and you wouldn't mind being its leader.

9. You expect to get married one day and to be the bread-winner.

10. You would see yourself as a bit of a failure if you didn't earn as much, and do as well, as your dad in your job eventually.

11. You find it embarrassing if others make 'excessive' displays of strong emotion.

12. You find it hard to be openly competitive and, if necessary, aggressive.

13. You think that winning an argument is much more important than seeing both sides of it.

14. You believe that women are naturally better suited than men to caring for children.

15. You like strong, independent women.

16. You prefer to be on top during sex.

17. You have been accused of being selfish in bed.

18. You have lots of female friends with whom sex doesn't come into it.

19. You *have* to have sex regularly or you begin to feel pent up and unfulfilled.

20. Some sexual partners have complained that you're not thrusting enough in bed.

Before scoring your diagnosis (see pages 103–4), you need to read the following introduction to the dominance dimension and the profiles of the different types.

Take a look at these two lists of qualities used to describe two opposite types of people:

Active	Passive
Initiates	Reluctant to initiate
Assertive	Unassertive
A direct, combative style of persuasion	An indirect, uncombative style of persuasion

Holds strong opinions and always expresses them forcefully	Not intense, diffident and very careful to avoid open conflict in conversation
Dominant	Submissive

The statements on the left sum up how males are traditionally supposed to behave; those on the right describe the traditional female role. But the interesting thing about dominance and submission in sexual relationships is that by no means all men and women conform to their traditional roles. There are as many dominant women as there are men, and as many men are submissive in style as women. Extremes of masculine or feminine behaviour are not actually caused by what you've got between your legs.

When we talk about 'dominance' or 'submission' in sexual relationships we're not talking about actual *control* or *power* in the battle of the sexes; we're talking about the styles by which people of both sexes express their aggression. The 'battle of the sexes' should really be called the 'battle of styles of aggression'. Indeed, there would be no war, let alone battles, if people always formed partnerships with compatible types.

Just because someone is submissive it doesn't mean that he or she doesn't control what happens; rather, submissive people tend to suppress their aggressive feelings when confronted with aggression from someone else. They tend not to weigh in with direct and open aggression towards others. But if you watch carefully, you'll see that it's by no means always the vehement, insistent person who seems to be in command that actually gets his or her way in the end. Submissive people have their own ways of exercising their will. Everybody knows loud, extroverted people whose partners can control them with a look or a gesture.

Whereas submissive types conceal their aggression, dominant types are exaggeratedly aggressive in style. They fear vulnerability and the feeling that there's nothing they can actually do – powerlessness. They react to this feeling by over-compensating in the opposite direction – by being overtly and forcefully aggressive in style.

Styles of dominance and submission are an important factor in the compatibility of two people. If you're a dominating woman, how do you get along with equally dominating men? If you're a submissive man, how do equally submissive women make you feel? The chances are that you don't find it easy to be together because the similarity of your styles produces a clash in the first case and a feeling of directionlessness and uncertainty in the second.

Many are the sexual triangles that have arisen through the incompatibility of a couple on the dominance dimension. Let's look at one such case.

Paul and Pauline got married after a whirlwind romance. Their friends called them 'the two Paulies', so similar were they in type, both very forceful and dominating.

The rows started during the honeymoon in Malta. They couldn't agree about the smallest thing. Beach versus pool? Wine versus beer? Early to bed versus late-night dancing? Anything and everything led to a clash.

Back at the office Paul met a new temp, a quiet, placid woman by the name of Sue. As the war at home got worse, Paul found Sue increasingly important to him: 'She *listened*. She didn't question everything I said. You could go out for a drink with her without having a major debate about where to go, where to sit when you got there, what to drink and when to leave.'

The inevitable happened, and now Sue and Paul are happily married.

This shows how important compatibility on the dominance dimension can be. The incompatibility in dominance between Paul and Pauline exacerbated the need in both of them for a more submissive partner, and, as it turned out, Paul was the first to find what was so desperately lacking in the form of Sue: a classic case of a dominance problem in the original couple creating a need that was fulfilled by a third party.

I have named the dominant man Big Boy (Big Boys Don't Cry) because of his reluctance to show his vulnerability, and I call dominant females Cosmo Women because of their thrusting, powerful tendencies. Submissive men I term Wimps, a word that I do not intend to be derogatory: it simply denotes a diffident, unassertive sort of man. Finally, Little Princess is the name for the submissive female type, indicating a woman who is used to relying on others and is unassertive.

The reader will have realized that the Big Boy and the Little Princess, and the Wimp and the Cosmo Woman, are compatible couples: dominance and submissiveness go together well – the attraction of opposites, if you will.

It may seem surprising, but submissive males and dominant females – the Wimp and Cosmo Woman – have in common a tendency to be rebels, to be individualists who are not actually antisocial but who believe strongly in being 'up-front' and speaking out and freeing themselves from the dictates of authority and conformism. On the other hand we find that dominant males and submissive females – the Big Boy and the Little Princess – share a tendency to uphold group values and norms, to reject antisocial individualism (although strongly in favour of the individual as such) and to feel that many things are best left unsaid. The types of dominant and submissive male and female are, interestingly enough, different in values, though similar in their style of aggression. This makes the two couples even more compatible. Not only do their dominance–submission styles avoid conflict and abrasion, but also Wimp–Cosmo couples and Big Boy–Little Princess couples have similar values.

The final feature of the types in this dimension is gender identity, sexual identity. This is not simply a matter of genitalia. The Big Boy is *such* a Big Boy because he wishes to show how masculine he is and to refute any possible accusation of being feminine even before it can be made. He is saying, 'I spell M-A-N and don't you dare suggest differently.' Likewise the Little Princess anticipates, and rejects, any claim that she has a masculine side by offering exaggeratedly feminine behaviour. In both cases their pronounced preference for society's way of saying 'I am male' or 'I am female' itself reveals that they are anxious about this.

On the other hand, the Wimp and Cosmo Woman are saying, 'Look at me. I don't conform to a sexual stereotype. I am ME.' Cosmo Woman's uninhibited expression of what society would call a 'masculine side' is her refutation of the idea that she is the passive female she was brought up to be. Likewise the Wimp's hatred for ostentatious male displays proves that he doesn't have to be macho to be male.

These differences provide yet another area of compatibility: the Wimp and Cosmo Woman see eye to eye about sexuality, and so do Big Boy and Little Princess. This suggests three fundamental reasons for their compatibility when it comes to style of aggression, values and sexual identity.

1. The Wimp and the Little Princess have a laid-back style, which means they do not get into rows when paired with the more aggressive Cosmo Woman and Big Boy respectively.

2. The Wimp and Cosmo Woman share an individualistic, up-front and rebellious philosophy, whereas the Big Boy and the Little Princess both believe in the group, are discreet and more private and are not rebels.

3. The Wimp and Cosmo Woman share an antipathy to sexual stereotypes imposed by society and are more than happy to behave in ways normally associated with the opposite sex. The Big Boy and the Little Princess, on the other hand, display exaggeratedly 'male' and 'female' styles respectively and, consequently, are well suited.

So you can see that it's important to find out whether you and your partner(s) are well suited on this dimension. What follows are profiles of the four types of personality. In each case a general profile is followed by a more specific account of how this type of person tends to behave in different circumstances. Read them all, and try to work out who's who on this dimension.

THE BIG BOY

Personality profile

Dimension: **Dominance**
Type: **Big Boy**
Position in triangle: **Any**
Famous examples of this sexual personality type: Brian Tilsley (*Coronation Street*), Jock Ewing (*Dallas*), Ian Botham, Clint Eastwood, Heathcliff (*Wuthering Heights*), Prince Andrew, Bruce Springsteen, William the Conqueror, Michael Heseltine, President Reagan, Paul Macartney and Ringo Starr, Sir Robin Day, Elvis Presley, Pete Beale and Simon Wicks (*EastEnders*)

General profile

Big Boys have conviction. They know who they are, and they know what's best for them. They're in control. And yet they have a vulnerable side which few may see. Big Boys *do* cry sometimes.

When they're out on a date it's a matter of courtesy and respect to pay for the drinks, the dinner and the cinema tickets, but they're reasonable about it. 'If the girl wants to pay, fine. I'm not a chauvinist, I don't like to make a big thing out of it. I often go Dutch these days.' The Big Boy is a romantic at heart: he likes to take a woman out, and he likes to treat her properly. He feels protective. Something of a diplomat, he's cool, he's got style; he's a bit of a charmer. And there are plenty of women who like those things in a man. His sort of girl is very supportive, and she's not the sort to compete with him. The Big Boy's highly developed competitive instincts are satisfied on the football field, in the squash court and at the work place. He's 'one of the lads', and indeed he has very few close female friends: his friends are almost exclusively male. He likes few things better than a boisterous night out with the boys.

And he has very masculine taste too. He's impressed by 'good design' in cars, cameras, hi-fi, for example. He likes quality, and he doesn't mind paying the price – 'It works out cheaper in the long run,' he will tell you. And that goes for his clothes: practical, classical, well made. Nothing too fancy. Smart and well turned-out, he's not ashamed of his class, and he's usually a credit to the company he keeps.

Occasionally he's the life and soul of the party. He goes to plenty of parties – he's gregarious. He likes to run with the pack, and although he would like to be the leader of it, he's prepared to wait his turn. He believes it's the selfish minority that always spoil it for the majority. On the whole what most people think is right. In the end he'll come down on the side of the authorities: 'It's just common sense really. I mean, most people agree – what would happen if everyone was antisocial?' At the same time your Big Boy believes strongly in the individual: 'Look at the great men of history . . . Behind every army there's a great general. In every great team there's a brilliant individualist.' And he'll fight for the rights of that individual – Big Boys won the war!

But the Big Boy's not intense. He likes to relax and have a few drinks. He'll let his hair down and maybe join in with his mates in a joke-telling session: 'How do you stop a queer from drowning? Take your foot off his head.' Cruel, he knows, but you've got to laugh. He enjoys a good laugh. But when he's had one too many he can be a bit of a braggart and a show-off. He regrets it the morning after, when he sees his clothes strewn anyhow on the floor and he remembers some of the things he said. He doesn't really like getting that legless – it's antisocial and you lose face. Still, great night, wasn't it?

But he's not irresponsible by nature. If there's a crisis – a fainting woman, for instance – he's a natural organizer, calming people down, sending for an ambulance and a glass of water. At such times he has Authority; he's a bit pompous and self-important, a bit of a school prefect, it might seem, but, as he puts it, 'Somebody's got to take responsibility.' And when he gets married he's not frightened to be a breadwinner. His wife may do the cooking and ironing (he pretends he can't do either) but in return he does the DIY and he brings home a regular wage. He's a hard worker but not obsessive. 'I put in the necessary hours because I want a certain standard of living – you know, comfortable enough.' Every generation of Big Boys slightly betters the one before. They like to give their children the best possible start in life.

Stomach aches, headaches, asthma, skin complaints, bad backs – all manner of aches and pains are the Big Boy's curse. He gets very worried about his health and sometimes, secretly, he fears that he is going to have a heart attack or a brain haemorrhage. But he's a great one for the stiff upper lip, and he won't let things get on top of him. He doesn't really like being vulnerable or emotional, and some things are best left unsaid. He respects people's privacy, and he'd rather not hear about your personal problems 'if you don't mind'. He could argue the hind legs off a donkey, his mum used to say, and he's difficult to pin down in an argument.

He totally disagrees with the statement 'Everybody's basi-cally bisexual' because, as he says, 'I can honestly say that I don't find other men's bodies attractive. The thought of two men kissing really turns me off.' And certainly he likes to be on top during sex. He finds women's bodies a bit of a mystery. 'The female orgasm' is not something he pretends to understand – that's for other people to pontificate about. He believes in deeds, not words, and he just lets his natural male drive take over, and whatever happens, happens. He's 'rarely had complaints', although some women have accused him of being a bit selfish behind his back.

Deeds, not words, an individual who works for the greater good, forceful yet vulnerable – that's the Big Boy. He believes in being a Man, and he's prepared to suffer in the attempt.

The triangular Big Boy

In the search for a wife, the Big Boy probably puts himself about a good bit, in the course of which he may become a third party. But on the whole he prefers single women, suitable for marriage. Once married, he is quite likely to be an unfaithful because 'Men have strong urges, you know, it's natural.' He can be very devious about his affairs. He doesn't want his wife to find out to save her feelings. He is not at all amused if his wife has an affair, however, and high dudgeon follows. But he doesn't like divorces either and is a believer in 'keeping together for the children'.

The faithful Big Boy

As a cause of infidelity on his partner's part, he can drive her to it by becoming predictable and boring: maybe he always wants the missionary position during sex; he tells the same stories and jokes again and again; he can spend too much time out with his male friends playing sports, drinking and generally being part of an exclusively masculine tribe in his spare time. He can cause problems by his reluctance to talk over emotional difficulties and by his inflexible insistence that they stay together 'for the sake of the children', come what may. Finally, he can be very blind to the danger of his wife going off with someone else – particularly if his best friend is involved. He 'just never would have guessed it' and afterwards is very resentful.

The unfaithful Big Boy

There is a tendency for him to see women as 'only good for one thing' and, if the chance arises at work, to take it. He has a need to prove his masculinity to himself and others and, if his wife goes off sex, may go elsewhere. He sees himself as an animal whose sex drive must be fulfilled regularly, and he reckons that whereas women are naturally faithful, men are not. There is a stag-party 'get 'em off' mentality when he's out with the boys, and this reinforces the idea that he's not really a man unless he's putting it about. So although he doesn't want to hurt his wife, he's liable to have flings, 'like any red-blooded male'. He's particularly susceptible to secretaries or subservient women at work – in fact, to any woman who'll massage his insecure masculine ego. He works hard at not getting caught and enjoys the game of thinking up excuses – it makes him feel clever and powerful. He believes it's his right to have it both ways.

The third-party Big Boy

Because he tends to have a wife or a girlfriend and because he doesn't like the idea of sharing another man's woman, he's not usually in this position. There is one common exception: his best friend's wife. This challenge is like an extension of the battles they fight on the tennis court and the golf course, and it can be as exciting to him as winning there. What he doesn't grasp, and what he would take a swing at you for pointing out, is that his desire for his best friend's wife is really yet another of the many examples of their intimacy. Women are chattels, after all, and why not use them as a means for communicating with your oldest and dearest friend too – and in a way that is so much more personal than hitting a tennis or a golf ball?

THE WIMP

Personality profile

Dimension: **Dominance**
Type: **Wimp**
Position in triangle: **Any**
Famous examples of this sexual personality type: Ken Barlow and Alf Roberts (*Coronation Street*), Bobby Ewing (*Dallas*), George Harrison, Mark Phillips, Gandhi, Bjorn Borg, George Smiley, Michael Crawford (*Some Mothers Do 'Ave 'Em*), Woody Allen, Lord Olivier, Prince Charles, Arthur Fowler and Lofty (*EastEnders*)

General profile

There's a new breed of man out and about today. He's called the Wimp. Ten years ago that would be a term of abuse, but no longer. Suddenly Wimping is OK. It's OK to be sensitive, open about your feelings, to see women as people rather than sex objects *and* to be male. But that doesn't make Wimps gay. Of course, there've always been men like this, but they've been forced to pretend that they're someone else until now. Even today, sadly, quite a few men still suffer from the pressure of a macho role that just isn't them. It's not only women who have been liberated by the changes of the recent past, for there are now many men who have been freed from their traditional role, and, who knows, in the next ten years we may witness a wimping revolution.

At work Wimps are realistic. They're sceptical and sensibly suspicious of the powers that be, the authorities. They know the way the system works, and it doesn't fool them, but they also know there's no alternative for the time being, so they use it for their own ends. All Wimps are highly competent at what they do and get very absorbed in it. But they invest energy only in achieving *their* goals; hierarchies and their values do not motivate them.

Some Wimps settle for a quiet life and a regular income. They often develop and exploit a particular technical skill or, if in a more mundane job, they develop a relaxed, comfortable attitude to their work that takes very little out of them – they're at peace with themselves at the end of the working day with plenty of energy left over to get on with more interesting things. They may work for a large corporation, but you'll never catch them saying, '*We*'ve really done very well this year'; more likely, they'll say, 'God, somebody must be making a bomb from this racket.'

Other Wimps are less phlegmatic. They see themselves at odds with the system, and they're working for the day when things will be on their own terms. They remain highly independent, often self-employed. At first, they are Wimps without a cause, rebels in search of a target; gradually they develop specific talents and, eventually, exploit them rather than being used by the system. These Wimps tend to be creative types, and the really successful ones create whole new alternative systems (Richard Branson's Virgin Records, *Time Out*, *Private Eye*). Wimps are highly ambitious and very hard-working, but in no way are they the ulcerated, *over-worked* businessmen whose hearts and arteries give such cause for concern. Their own health and peace of mind are their first priority, for they realize that money, power and status do not in themselves bring happiness.

For the same reason Wimps do not allow arguments or rows to raise their blood pressure. They're the diplomats who tactfully persuade both parties to see each other's point of view or at least to agree to differ. They may well be pro-feminist, for example, but in the face of a heated argument about the issue they won't make matters worse by weighing in heavily on the side they favour. Instead they'll be quick to point out reasons for holding the opposing view. Wimps will always put smooth and pleasant social transactions ahead of an idea, for which there is always a place: 'This really isn't the time to argue about it. So why don't you both have another drink? By the way, have you seen the new Roeg movie?' The Wimp is not loud and he's not shy, but he can be assertive when appropriate and, above all, he's easy-going and relaxed. He finds it very difficult to get angry, and his hateful feelings are very rarely expressed openly – always indirectly, tor-tuously even.

And when he relaxes he likes to tell a few jokes. 'How many folk singers does it take to change a light bulb? Six – one to change the bulb and five to sing about how good the old bulb was.' They're gentle jokes, unlikely to upset anyone (except maybe the odd folk singer!). Spastic and cripple jokes are definitely not his style.

Just as he shies away from violent arguments, so the Wimp avoids competitive sport, especially team games: 'I can't think of a worse way to spend a Saturday afternoon than getting your head down in a scrum with sixteen sweaty lads covered in mud, pushing each other about.' He does like to keep fit but sets his own targets, perhaps increasing the distance of his daily run or the number of lengths down at the baths. If he does get involved in a competitive sport, it's out of the mainstream – fencing, basket ball, badminton. You see, it's not the aggression he dislikes about sport – it's having to be one of the lads. Getting pissed in the bar afterwards (a few drinks is enough for the Wimp, he knows when to stop), 'mooning' your bottom on the coach, all that leering at the girls: 'I went to one of those rugby dos once. The captain drank five pints of beer in two and a half minutes and sicked it up all over the scrum-half. He was stripped naked and left in a phone box. It's all so false. You get the feeling they're just pretending to have fun, showing off to each other. Childish, really.' The Wimp loathes any situation, at work or play, which challenges his individuality. He won't subordinate it at any price. He prizes it too highly.

As far as technology is concerned, it's either got to be practical or 'stylish' or both: 'Those Citroën 2CVs may look odd, but they've got character. And they're very low on petrol and easy to maintain.' He's not really into car mechanics, but he may have been to night school or bought a manual of car maintenance, so that he sort of knows what's what. The latest hi-fi or camera doesn't turn him on. He just wants things to work.

The appearance of things or putting on appearances is not for him, and it shows in his domestic life. His surroundings are comfortable and homely; his clothes are individualistic but neither flashy nor obsessively smart and clean. In the kitchen (it's not particularly clean or tidy, but it's not squalid either – no cockroaches) he may leave the washing-up till tomorrow, but he can cook and he doesn't mind admitting to it: 'I've added a little extra garlic. It was a bit bland last time.' The same goes for ironing, 'although it's a wonder what you achieve just by hanging them up as soon as they've been washed'.

The Wimp is realistic, if somewhat diffident and laid-back,

in his friendships and love life. He can be close to women without wanting to sleep with them: 'We're just good friends. You don't have to have sex just because you're a bloke and she's a woman. You do have a choice, you know.' He will talk openly with his male friends about his personal life, and they express affection for each other freely (they don't think it's poofy to embrace when they part, for example). This closeness may date back to adolescence when the Wimp and his best friend would play hooky from the football field to spend long afternoons listening to cassettes and talking about sex and the meaning of life.

The Wimp doesn't 'give women one' or 'get his end away'. He cringes when he hears this sort of talk, although he may secretly share the same sentiments. Instead, he goes dutch on a date and may or may not end up in bed with the woman, depending on *both* their moods.

He likes kids and looks forward to the day when he will have some to care for. He makes a good father (as far as the kids are concerned – no stern disciplinarian, he) and he doesn't mind sharing the care – he sees nothing cissy about changing a nappy or powdering a baby's bottom. He's not crazy about having to be a breadwinner, but he buckles down manfully if that's how it turns out. Wimps don't like weak, soppy, clinging women. They like their women to have a bit of get up and go. Yet, strangely enough, a highly feminine, seductive 'dumb blonde' may produce lustful fantasies, although these are rapidly dismissed: 'Of course, underneath it all she's totally superficial. I can never find anything to talk about with her.' He realizes that fancying her is what he was brought up to do: 'Glossy magazines and page three – it's rammed down your throat all the time.' But, for all his awareness, it's an uncomfortable fact that she still produces a stirring in his loins. After all, every male is raised a Big Boy.

Wimps are firmly heterosexual, although the odd homosexual thought may have crossed their mind and, in some cases, been translated into practice. They'd agree that we're all basically bisexual but only up to a point.

In bed they won't make a big thing about orgasms, their own or their partner's: 'Caressing, touching, feeling really sensuous all over – it's great. It's not just about a big bang.' They like an uninhibited, active partner, and there's no holds barred. They don't feel they've got to be on top, and on the whole their partners appreciate them. Some women find them a little too laid-back and complain that Wimps don't push hard enough in the final furlong. The Wimp shrugs his shoulders: 'What do you think I am, for God's sake? A horse?'

One of the few who is not one of the lads, a system hater and a system maker, sensitive and diffident, tomorrow's man in yesterday's world – that's the Wimp.

The triangular Wimp

On the whole, the Wimp's relaxed, easy-going personality and his preference for diplomacy over confrontation make for stable and relatively harmonious relationships. However, his diffidence can lead to trouble under certain conditions, as can the slight ambiguity of his gender. If he does get involved in a threesome, he's less likely than other types to prolong the agony – he knows when to call it a day, although it isn't his style to do so dramatically or aggressively (he calls a spade a gardening implement).

The faithful Wimp

He can be the cause of his partner's infidelity in several ways. First, if she is obviously in danger of going off with someone else, his diffidence may not let him protest enough to prevent it from happening. An affair that disrupts the couple may ensue, and it may be too late to repair the damage later on. Secondly, his partner may feel rejected or insulted by his diffidence and seek an alternative lover to make him put in more effort. Thirdly, he may be the object of covert and displaced homosexual longings – a friend may have an affair with his girlfriend as an indirect means of getting involved with him, and his own desire for this to happen might stop him from intervening sufficiently.

The unfaithful Wimp

The Wimp's diffidence may make him one of those 'what the eye does not see . . .' types of partner. He's not too bothered if she's unfaithful to him, so long as it doesn't affect their relationship and he doesn't have to know, and he may reckon that a bit of infidelity on his part doesn't really do any harm either.

His bisexuality means he often likes a woman who is active and quite aggressive but not too much. So he may begin to roam if his partner is either too aggressive (to the point of being a bully) or too passive (to the point of being a doormat).

His diffidence also means he is relatively easy to persuade into bed – a dominating, charismatic woman may well be able to override his attempts to stay faithful if she is persuasive enough. He might just go along with it because he's not that bothered either way.

Likewise, if he has a partner who actively encourages infidelity, he may well be persuaded to go ahead, given the fact that he's not averse to sex and not dogmatic about the need to remain faithful.

The third-party Wimp

He's not motivated to chase women by the fact that they already have a partner because he's not very competitive. However, he may find himself in bed with the partners of his close friends, thereby indirectly expressing his attraction for his friends.

Otherwise he is likely to become a third party only because the unfaithful persuades him to. The fact that he doesn't feel terribly worried about betraying the faithful makes this relatively easy for a persistent unfaithful. It's not that he wants to betray other men, it's just that he reckons it's their problem rather than his, if he thinks about it at all.

THE LITTLE PRINCESS

Personality profile

Dimension: **Dominance**
Type: **Little Princess**
Position in triangle: **Any**
Famous examples of this sexual personality type: Gail
 Tilsley (*Coronation Street*), Miss Ellie Ewing (*Dallas*),
 Princess Diana, Marilyn Monroe, Barbara Cartland and
 her heroines, Selina Scott, Diana Ross, Debby Harry
 (*Blondie*), Nancy Reagan, Kathy Beale and Sharon Watts
 (*EastEnders*)

General profile

Little Princesses appear girlish and feminine on the surface,
but there's quite a woman to be reckoned with when you get
to know them well. They may not be in the driving seat, but
they certainly know how to get from A to B. They don't deny
that it's a man's world, but they know that behind every great
man there's a woman.

Little Princesses have liked romances since they were
small. Although they may smile about it now, tales of dashing
men who sweep women off their feet have always struck a
chord in their hearts (Mills and Boon novels, *Lace* or, for the
more literary, *Wuthering Heights*). They couldn't help but
be moved by the fairytale transformation from Cinders to
Cinderella of Lady Di.

And one day their prince will come. Little Princesses like
to have boyfriends, and if a romance turns sour, they're quick
to take a new lover. It's not that they're addicted to men, it's
just that they like to have a man in their life.

And it's a particular sort of man. There's a lot to be said for
old-fashioned chivalry: 'After all, what's wrong with having a
door held open for you or being offered a seat on a crowded

train? It's just good manners.' And if you're out on a date, a Little Princess will often go Dutch, but if you offer to pay, she's not going to argue. She likes to be pampered a bit – it's good to feel looked after. She likes her man to look smart – not flash, just quietly stylish. She can spot a man with class a mile off, and although she knows that money can't buy you love, she's not exactly put off if he's got a bob or two: there's nothing worse than penny-pinching on a date.

But if she lets men pay occasionally, that doesn't mean that she thinks they're the boss: 'it's obvious that women are in charge really. Men are like little boys. If you pander to them, they think they're in control.' Her men always turn up on time for dates; if not, they get short shrift. She, on the other hand, is less punctual – it's a woman's prerogative.

So the Little Princess tends to have a man in her life. That's not to say she doesn't have female friends, but her man comes first, and if that means changing an appointment with her best friend because something better has come up – like a man, for instance! – then all's fair. And her best friend probably understands because she's not as attractive as the Little Princess. But there are advantages to having one as a friend because Little Princesses are popular, and they often draw men like magnets. And they always want to be part of the most impressive social scene available. Through her men the Little Princess establishes good contacts: 'I used to eat here with Gerry. I'm sure we'll get a table'; 'It's all right – I know the man who runs Moros. We should get in for free.' Good reason to have her as a friend, even if she flaunts it a bit: Little Princesses like to make you feel they're exclusive.

Understandably, she hasn't got many close female friends because they tend to envy her and to bitch about her. That's hardly her fault: 'Can I help it if they don't watch their weight and don't know how to dress?' She's not a woman's woman, and if other women feel competitive, that's their problem. The Little Princess *is* actuely aware of what other women look like: 'You just don't wear those trousers when you have such big hips.' The Little Princess will always look better:

she knows how to carry it off. She's not just a pretty face, though; if it does come to a competition for a man, there's none wiser and few can match her guile.

Little Princesses dress smartly and neatly, with class. Her clothes are very feminine, with classic styling. Sometimes, for a special party when the mood takes her, she looks really sexy but always in a 'tasteful' way. At other times, she loves to wear a stylish evening dress, dramatic but not ostentatious (it causes a stir when she arrives). The Little Princess likes to stand out from the crowd, but she never forgets that there are limits. The approval of her set is important, and although she knows that she has the power to dominate a room full of men, she's careful not to overdo it. Occasionally she becomes outspoken and blatantly lecherous when she gets tiddly, but this is very rare – she's careful to watch how much she drinks because she needs to be in control of herself and she can't abide coarse, blatant behaviour. Normally she feels that a lot of things are best left unsaid. Just as she prefers a neat bedroom (even though the clothes may have been chucked anyhow into the drawers) or a shiny clean cooker (although what's beneath it wouldn't bear close inspection), so she prefers good behaviour (even if the real feelings are anything but) and polite language (although her real thoughts are far from). Talk of periods, constipation, people farting and burping, rotting food and messy medical problems are not her scene. In social situations she'd prefer to forget that there are bodies beneath clothes, and in bed she'd rather not know that there are bodily fluids beneath skin. Her scene is civilization, glamour, the social niceties.

The Little Princess is one of life's consumers rather than breadwinners. She loves shopping far more than she loves working. Not that she's lazy – it's just that she's not madly ambitious in her career. After all, she's always known she wanted children. So as she's got older she's turned into a useful cook (she loves going out to restaurants or grabbing a take-away, but she has also learned how to do it herself) and she's become increasingly keen on keeping the house tidy.

(When she was younger her room could be a real mess, but it was never actually squalid – there were never mice.)

She loves small talk and gossip, and she's good at it. The first time you meet her she laughs a lot, even at things that aren't funny – but that's just nerves. She has a good sense of humour, which tends to be deployed at other people's expense – wicked, but you've got to laugh. Sometimes the joke's on her, though. The captivated audience of men to whom she tells her long and involved stories, don't find her foolish at all and really enjoy them.

The Little Princess is a woman and she knows it. She would laugh scornfully at the idea we're all basically bisexual. What she likes is a man who is a real man: he does the work in bed and she enjoys it. She knows she's good at giving men pleasure, although there are limits to what she'll let him do or do for him. Can you blame her? Some things are not the stuff of true romance. Also men can be very selfish, can't they? Particularly the sort of men she ends up with, but she's not one to complain to his face because it's not the sort of thing you talk about.

Seductive yet old-fashioned, romantic yet realistic, pliant yet in control, skin-deep yet full of guile – that's the Little Princess. She's a character from a romantic novel, and she's as hard-headed as they come.

The triangular Little Princess

As soon as she can, she gets a boyfriend, and for the rest of her life she feels incomplete without one. Up until marriage she has serious, discreet affairs with potential husbands. This means she doesn't waste much time on married men unless there's a real possibility of a good catch. She wants as much class and cash in her man as she can attract: her face is her fortune. Much of her energy is devoted to making other women envious, so her man must be the sort that they will covet. Once she's got him in the bag, she's very reluctant to let go, so there is a tendency to be a faithful. Messing about as a third party, or infidelity, could wreck all her hard work.

However, there are conditions under which either of these may occur.

The faithful Little Princess

In her teens and early twenties she's playing the field, so at this point, unless she strikes gold immediately, she's only waiting until something better comes along before moving on. However, once she's chosen her man, all her energies go into getting him to the church on time, and infidelity would hardly be a way to achieve that (except in extreme cases, where she might do it to make him jealous by making sure he finds out). Once married, she turns a blind eye to her husband's indiscretions – the chances are she has married the sort of man who's discreet about his peccadilloes, and so long as it doesn't humiliate her, she's prepared to put up with it. 'Boys will be boys,' she says to herself. This doesn't mean she's happy about it – far from it: she watches him like a hawk and tries to keep tabs on him as much as she can – but she's too crafty to make a big fuss. She uses infidelity to get what she wants by making him feel guilty. But if a real threat comes along, she fights tooth and nail, and probably very effectively, unless he's found an even prettier Little Princess.

She is most likely to provoke her husband to roam by becoming dull to him: she may be too inactive in bed, too repetitive and tediously petty in her preoccupations out of it, or he may feel that she should 'take up an interest'. But, on the whole, she's too aware of the pitfalls to let these things happen and quick to spot the danger; she will adapt herself to be more interesting to him. Of course, she confides to her close friends, it's she who's really in charge, but you've got to let men think it's they who wear the pants.

The unfaithful Little Princess

She's not keen on infidelity herself – although she loves gossiping about that of others with her friends – because it threatens her carefully arranged life. However, there are three conditions that can bring it about. First, a man who is highly skilled at making her feel like a character in a romance may just do the trick. It is part of her self-image that she could dupe her husband and have a sneaky affair with a wonderful prince if she wanted to, and if the right prince makes all the right moves, then she may do so. But he's got to get it exactly right – particularly the timing. He must choose a moment in her marriage when she's a bit fed-up. Secondly, she may find that her husband's class and income don't quite match her ambition or, if they do, that he is really an ungentlemanly brute whom she is not prepared to tolerate. In these circumstances she will consider investing her assets elsewhere, and the buyer who makes the right kind of offer could be in luck. Of course, someone who is extremely wealthy and classy is always in with a chance with any Little Princess if he plays his cards right – unless, that is, she actually *is* a princess, in which case he must be royalty as well! Thirdly, the Little Princess likes to prove her attractiveness to men on a regular basis. Normally she does this by flirting but not actually delivering, but in exceptional circumstances (for example, if her husband goes off sex for a bit), she may have a fling to prove her point.

Generally speaking, though, she is sufficiently frightened by the prospect of being disenfranchised through divorce to avoid risky affairs, especially (as is often the case) if she has married a man who believes in his right to be unfaithful but to expect fidelity from her.

The third-party Little Princess

As a young woman she's prepared to be in this position if it will get her somewhere – she's happy to get another woman's husband if he really is the goods. She doesn't mind showing off her pulling power either. But set against these things are the gut feeling she has that being a third party is messy and risky; it would probably mean being hidden away, and she wouldn't get all the respect and power that comes with being a wife. Above all, she would run the risk of being branded a scarlet woman.

On the whole, then, the Little Princess is against this role unless she's fallen on hard times, perhaps as the victim of a divorce.

THE COSMO

Personality profile

Dimension: **Dominance**
Type: **Cosmo**
Position in triangle: **Any**
Famous examples of this sexual personality type: Rita
    Fairclough (*Coronation Street*), Pam Ewing (*Dallas*),
    Queen Elizabeth I, Anna Ford, Princess Anne, Germaine
    Greer, Princess Margaret, Joan of Arc, Jane Fonda,
    Pauline and Michelle Fowler (*EastEnders*)

General profile

Cosmos don't take life lying down. They're the new breed of woman born of the social turmoil of the 1960s. They have both feet firmly on the ground, and they keep pushing at home, at work and at play. All too often they can appear selfish, but they know that if they're going to be any use to anyone, they've got to put number one first. They're continually fighting the traditional role of women in themselves and in those around them.

Cosmos don't feel they have to have a boyfriend all the time: 'I can feel a whole person without a man in my life.' If they do get married, they'll keep up a separate life with friends. Cosmos tend to have a lot of female friends and, sometimes, gay men friends.

The Cosmo likes her men to be laid-back, easy-going types. Money and status don't particularly impress her in themselves. Competitive, dominant men soon find themselves at odds with a Cosmo. However, sometimes she has yearnings to be looked after, perhaps when pressures become too great. After all, nearly every girl is brought up to be a Little Princess not a Cosmo, so it's not surprising she has the occasional 'lapse'. But she overrules such feelings in favour of a man who's not going to cramp her style.

Cosmos tend not to get pinned down until their late twenties or early thirties; until then they generally see themselves as free agents even if they're living with someone: 'It's not that I don't love you; it's just that I'm not ready to make a commitment.' Some men find this frustrating and accuse the Cosmo of opportunism, but when she reaches the right age with the right man then *she'll decide* she's ready for such an important move. Even when she does take this decision, she may indulge in the odd one-night stand (rather than a full-blown affair), just to exercise her freedom. She's realistic and level-headed about the prospect of her partner having an affair.

Besides, such behaviour stops a man getting too dependent. Cosmos get angry with men who want to behave like little boys. They don't see themselves as heavily maternal types. Some Cosmos may well say in their early twenties that they'll never have children. Those who decide to do so may seriously consider being a single parent. Some Cosmos come to terms with the idea of marriage, although it's normally to ease pressure from the in-laws or for financial reasons rather than because of a belief in its sanctity. Most Cosmos expect to go back to work soon after the birth of their children.

At work the Cosmo is busy, hard-working and pushy. Very competent at what she's chosen to do, she may be highly ambitious and, if so, will sacrifice treasured principles as she moves onwards and upwards. On the whole, though, Cosmos are not corporate women; they have independent ideas of their own. So they tend to find their own niche in the system and to run it very effectively – the comprehensive school that's trying a new method, the innovative law centre, the magazine with a difference. Cosmos have problems dealing with authority.

And they can be slightly abrupt at work and may be seen as a bit sour and earnest, but that's just because they take it seriously. When they let their hair down at the office party their witty and sarcastic side shows itself: 'She's not so bad after all, is she? I had trouble with her at first but I really like her now.' The Cosmo makes another friend.

The Cosmo is a champion at office politics. Realistically suspicious of the behaviour of colleagues and bosses, she knows how to put herself across when it's her turn to speak at a meeting. Although she believes passionately in openness and in calling spades spades, she knows there's a time and place for everything – she can be very tactful and crafty when she needs to be at work and at home.

She may make her own clothes, but if she's too busy, she'll buy off the peg. She'll be very critical of mass-produced items and will be the first to point out poor stitching and low quality. As they grow older Cosmos begin to realize that it's better to buy expensive, designer clothes: 'It works out cheaper in the long run.' Her taste is individualistic. Her wardrobe reveals many different styles, from sporty gear to evening dress. She has clothes for every occasion.

Cosmos are not chained to the kitchen sink. They have little interest in food or in cooking it themselves. They are quite content to grab a take-away or a healthy sandwich in a bar. However, when it comes to eating out, they take a real pleasure in selecting restaurants (especially of the ethnic variety) and particularly relish the social aspect of the occasion. When Cosmos do decide to entertain at home their dishes will reflect their usual flair and panache (particularly Cosmos in their thirties and forties).

Generally, they're in favour of healthy eating and exercise (aerobics, jogging). Some smoke and drink quite heavily, especially the young ones and those who are headed for the top. Others denounce such self-destructive practices with vehemence. Whatever their lifestyle, all Cosmos believe in thinking positive: 'You can't let things get on top of you. What's the use in getting depressed?' If smoking or drinking or weight becomes a problem, they're happy to sort it out in a self-help group.

The Cosmo's disposition is cheerful, relaxed and out-going. At the same time, she is assertive, firm, tough and decisive. She's not dogmatic, and she can see when she's wrong, but it can be hard to get a word in edgeways when the subject is near to her heart. She has a no-nonsense, prag-matic, matter-of-fact, realistic philosophy. She's read and adapted to suit herself such books as *Superwoman*, *The Female Eunuch* and *Having It All*. She is competitive, but not threateningly so, in her earnest pursuit of her goal, which is power before money or status – she wants to run her own niche. Overall, this mix of characteristics creates a constant tension between getting what she wants and her gentleness and warmth.

That we are all basically bisexual Cosmos would agree, but with the qualification that they are more hetero- than homosexual. Some may have experimented with their own sex, and many, although they are firmly heterosexual, will admit that it's crossed their minds once or twice.

Cosmos like sex (though some are too busy for it). They've worked hard to free themselves of inhibitions and have explored the possibilities with many different partners. They have a down-to-earth, functional attitude: 'After all, it *is* a physical act.' They enjoy their orgasms, and they don't mind being on top. They want to play an active part in the proceedings, and they're willing to try most things.

A lover yet a loner, assertive yet relaxed, gentle yet tough, today's woman in yesterday's world – that's the Cosmo woman. She looks after number one but, as she gets older, softens and cares for others too. Above all, she's truly cosmopolitan.

The triangular Cosmo

A great divide exists between Cosmo woman before the age of 30 and afterwards. On the whole, she doesn't get married young or, if she does, she may well get divorced because she feels trapped by its constraints. During her twenties she is very busy, probably working hard in a career or in activities outside work, like local politics, sport, artistic activities, community work and so forth. However, eventually she is faced with the possibility of being childless and alone for the rest of her life, and she isn't getting any younger. At this point, after much agonizing, she probably decides to settle down with one man. She still likes to be independent, but she has come to recognize that she needs someone else to share her life with.

During her twenties Cosmo woman tends not to be a faithful. She is more likely to have an open relationship or to be a free agent altogether, in which case she will probably find herself in the role of third party every so often. But snatching other people's men doesn't give her a thrill in itself – on the whole she is sympathetic to other women rather than competitive with them. Her competitiveness is at work (and here, she doesn't care about the sex of the adversary) in particular and with men in general – she knows she's as good as they are, and she's out to prove her point.

The faithful Cosmo

In her twenties the most likely reason for her being in this position is that she is too hard-working to have the time and energy for flings and wants the stable support of one person as a back-up to her gruelling life. A supportive, friendly, unchallenging man will fit this bill best because she can be very argumentative and difficult at times, and her partner needs to be a bit of a diplomat. As a faithful, if she is the cause of dissatisfaction in the relationship, it is probably this slightly domineering tendency or the fact that she's so busy which leads her man to seek another lover. The other possibility is that she has a very close bond with a female friend (of whom she has many), and this is expressed through sharing her partner.

In later life she tends to be a reliable and constructive partner who is a very efficient homemaker. So long as she has settled with the right man, things run smoothly. She may not even be too bothered if he has discreet affairs because she's got her own life and she doesn't think it's the end of the world – just so long as it doesn't disturb their life together.

The unfaithful Cosmo

While young, she quickly starts to feel cramped and to want her freedom if the relationship makes many demands on her. If she's involved with a bullying man or a chauvinist pig, sooner or later she finds a more liberated and laid-back partner and, after a bit, probably chucks her original partner quite abruptly. At this point in her life she soon realizes that life's too short to be tied to one man; she may have elaborate political or other justifications for this view. At this time too she regards herself as an experimenter and wants to try out all sorts of relationships. If she's a hard worker, she may well have many affairs with colleagues. Some of them don't do her career prospects any harm either (although she'd be furious if you pointed this out!).

Later on in her life, when settled, she may be prone to the occasional fling, so long as it doesn't risk destroying her stable set-up. However, if she has settled with an inappropriate partner, she is not afraid to acknowledge this to herself and to do something about it. But she won't be rash or impulsive; she'll make a sensible new beginning either on her own or, after careful consideration, with a new man.

The third-party Cosmo

In her twenties, she may well find herself having an affair with a married man, quite probably one she has met at work. However, her motive is not to hurt his wife – if the Cosmo thinks about her, she regrets this aspect of the matter and thinks less of her lover to the extent that he is heartless towards his wife. She doesn't get bogged down in this affair and, if it becomes frustrating or awkward, will rather break it off than continue. If he starts talking about leaving his wife,

Cosmo Woman discourages him, and she certainly doesn't go on at him to leave his wife for herself.

Later on, if she has chosen to remain single (a rare event) or has had a divorce (more common), she may have affairs with married men. But, again, their marital status is incidental to her. As a single Cosmo in her thirties and afterwards, she has probably decided to avoid intense entanglements, and there is a pragmatic, 'we're both adults' feel to relationships. The minute a man starts getting weepy or over-involved, she pulls away. The same considerations would go for affairs she might have with married men if she is herself married – unless she is seeking a new partner, in which case she will be highly organized and realistic about getting her man.

FOR WOMEN: THE COSMO–LITTLE PRINCESS DIAGNOSIS

Your answers to the test on page 73 will reveal that you are either a Cosmo (C) or a Little Princess (LP). Check them against the list below to diagnose your sexual personality type. Count up the scores for each type. The highest score indicates your tendency on the dominance dimension.

1.	Yes = C	No = LP
2.	Yes = LP	No = C
3.	Yes = LP	No = C
4.	Yes = C	No = LP
5.	Yes = LP	No = C
6.	Yes = C	No = LP
7.	Yes = LP	No = C
8.	Yes = C	No = LP
9.	Yes = C	No = LP
10.	Yes = LP	No = C
11.	Yes = C	No = LP
12.	Yes = LP	No = C
13.	Yes = LP	No = C
14.	Yes = LP	No = C

15.	Yes = C	No = LP
16.	Yes = C	No = LP
17.	Yes = LP	No = C
18.	Yes = C	No = LP
19.	Yes = LP	No = C
20.	Yes = C	No = LP

FOR MEN: THE BIG BOY–WIMP DIAGNOSIS

Your answers to the test on page 74 will reveal that you are either a Big Boy (BB) or a Wimp (W). Check them against the list below to diagnose your sexual personality type. Count up the scores for each type. The highest score indicates your tendency on the dominance dimension.

1.	Yes = BB	No = W
2.	Yes = BB	No = W
3.	Yes = BB	No = W
4.	Yes = W	No = BB
5.	Yes = BB	No = W
6.	Yes = BB	No = W
7.	Yes = BB	No = W
8.	Yes = BB	No = W
9.	Yes = BB	No = W
10.	Yes = BB	No = W
11.	Yes = BB	No = W
12.	Yes = W	No = BB
13.	Yes = W	No = BB
14.	Yes = W	No = BB
15.	Yes = W	No = BB
16.	Yes = BB	No = W
17.	Yes = BB	No = W
18.	Yes = W	No = BB
19.	Yes = BB	No = W
20.	Yes = W	No = BB

5 THE MAP OF YOUR SEXUAL LANDSCAPE

The time has come for you to put together what you've found out so far.

Take a blank piece of paper and write down the following categories on it:

Sexual personality type
Second tendency
Third tendency

You have done three tests so far, in each of which you got a score out of 20. Write the name of type for which you had the highest score beside the first category, 'Sexual Personality type'. Your second highest score indicates your 'second tendency' type: Your third highest score shows your 'third tendency' type. Write in both of these too. If, for example, you scored 14 as a Cosmo on the dominance dimension, 13 as a Splitter on the lust dimension and 11 as a Bully on the insecurity dimension, then you are a Cosmo with a Splitter second tendency and a Bully third tendency. (If you have the same score for two of the tests, you must decide which is the most potent tendency.)

Now you know who you are in the relationship stakes. But what about your partner?

To establish the sexual personality type of your partner, all you have to do is to take the diagnostic tests on his or her behalf or, if possible, get him or her to do them, which is more fun.

Once you have both scores on the tests, you can establish the basic map of your relationship. For example, it might be:

You		Your partner	
SPT	Cosmo	**SPT**	Clinger
Second tendency	Splitter	Second tendency	Wimp
Third tendency	Bully	Third tendency	Donor

If you are a member of a sexual triangle, then you can expand this map by scoring the third party on the tests as well or getting him or her to do them if this is practical. This will complete the map of your sexual landscape.

Now you are ready to find out whether you are with the right partner and what the risks of infidelity are with particular types of third party.

PART II

Predicting Infidelity: a Complete Guide to the
Twenty-eight Types of Couple

6 THE CAUSES OF INFIDELITY

The sexual infidelity that gives rise to triangles is caused by a combination of three factors.

1. Distorted desires on the lust dimension. One or both members of the couple confuse their current relationship with one that they had with their parents when they were small children. One partner encourages, or does not prevent, the other's interest in third parties, and the other partner becomes increasingly excited by the prospect of sex with relative strangers and turned off by the familiar partner. This creates the opportunity for a third party to snatch the potentially unfaithful member of the original couple from the faithful one.

2. Irrational fears on the insecurity dimension. An unrealistic anxiety, on the part of one or both lovers, that they will be abandoned or are being rejected leads them to behave in an unpleasant or disturbing way. This destabilizes the relationship and creates the risk that one of them will take a lover who makes him or her feel safe or as an act of revenge for an imagined slight.

3. Incompatibility on the dominance dimension. Clashes between the faithful and the unfaithful in styles of aggression or values or sexual identity – or all three – lead to dissatisfaction and disagreement and make the couple vulnerable to a third party whose compatibility with one or other partner is greater.

DISTORTED DESIRES ON THE LUST DIMENSION

Let us turn to the first major cause of infidelity.

When it comes to what sort of person we desire, we all have our personal preferences, shaped by our families. At the same time our general ideas about attractiveness are shaped by society through the ideal images of male and female beauty that are projected all day, every day, by the media. So what is deemed attractive in one society is not in another, and in the same way families cultivate different preferences.

There is such a thing as undistorted desire. Take two men standing together at a party. Enter a tall, thin, miniskirted young woman. 'Blimey, she's gorgeous,' one says. 'Yeah, gorgeous,' comes the reply. She corresponds to their idea of what's generally considered to be gorgeous. They've never met her, and so far it's nice and simple. Take two women at the same party. Observing the scene, they agree that the unknown man in the corner with the well-fitting jeans, athletic figure and clean-cut look is just their type.

Things get more complex when the men actually talk with the gorgeous woman, or when the athletic hunk is engaged in conversation by the women. The gorgeous woman is no longer a thing in a miniskirt; the hunk is no longer a tailor's dummy in well-fitting jeans. Each has a personality, which will affect how the partygoers feel about the pretty/handsome face and body. Likes and dislikes will develop within a minute of the start of the conversation. First impressions, based on minimal evidence, will slot the new acquaintance into categories that pre-existed the meeting and are hard and fast. Like moulds filled with quick-drying cement, each will be assigned a personality that will soon require a pneumatic drill to dislodge. On the basis of their early impressions, the partygoers relate to what they have decided the gorgeous woman and the hunk are like.

From the moment we open our mouths there is distortion in our view of each other, and in all normal relationships we struggle along, hearing and seeing only what we expect the concrete dummies of our expectation to say and do. Using the person standing before us, we transplant on to them images from the past to create as close as possible a match between the original and the dummy. But these are inevitable distortions, the price we pay for having to use our past as the basis for making choices in the present. They are the relatively straightforward distortions with which we choose objects of desire.

Matters become problematical when desire is caused largely by the presence of a triangle in itself. Transplanting from the past, the Splitter's desire for a familiar partner dries up and is channelled towards an unfamiliar third party. Whatever the objective merits of new lovers as compared with those of present partners, Splitters desire them above all because they are not familiar and because they are forbidden. However much the third party believes it is the unfaithful's beauty and special personality that are responsible for the lust, it is the fact that the Splitter already has a lover, and that he or she is prohibited, that is crucial. And the Donor's inability to prevent all this from happening, or even his or her encouragement of it, is related to the fact that the situation is triangular. All three are in the grip of the eternal triangle of the family from which each originally came.

Distorted desires cause triangles, alongside incompatibility and insecurity. Splitting destroys the sex life of the original couple and creates the need for a third party; donating increases the likelihood of the unfaithful having an affair; and snatching is just that – snatching. If one partner is a Splitter, a Donor or a Snatcher, a triangle is very likely.

Of course, a Donor cannot donate a partner who isn't interested in having an affair; a Splitter can't have an affair if no third party is prepared to do so; and a Snatcher cannot snatch from a couple unless the unfaithful is prepared to go along with the scheme. But if any one of these individuals is really pushing for it, he or she will get what they want. Very few couples are so compatible and secure that there is no occasion when a Donor cannot put unavoidable temptation in the way of a partner. At some point, incompatibility or insecurity will destabilize them enough for the Donor's partner to be tempted by opportunities for infidelity created by the Donor. Likewise, if Snatchers have any nous at all, they should have no trouble in finding a vulnerable couple and effecting a seduction. And there would have to be something badly wrong with any Splitter who was unable to find a willing third party of some description – apart from anything else, he or she only has to find one of the many Snatchers in search of an unfaithful!

IRRATIONAL FEARS ON THE INSECURITY DIMENSION

Now let's look at the second factor that causes sexual infidelity.

Most people don't like being bullied by their lover. You can do without being pushed around, harangued and attacked for no good reason. Life's too short.

Few people want a lover who clings. Questions about where you're going to be today, unreasonable demands, constant requests for comfort rather than sex – who needs them?

Bully and Clinger tendencies are produced by irrational fears, and they destabilize relationships, increasing the likelihood of infidelity. The expectation is of being rejected or abandoned, and where these tendencies are strong it's very hard to convince someone that neither is happening. They won't listen to what you say; all they hear is rejection or abandonment. And the worst thing is that Bully and Clinger tendencies bring about the very rejection or abandonment they fear. There are two classic cycles.

The Bully cycle

BULLY: Why do you always do that to me? It's because you don't really love me, isn't it? Eh?

PARTNER: No, really, I do love you. Come on, let's change the subject.

BULLY: There you go again, giving me the brush-off, changing the subject. You bastard – you're so bloody self-centred. Pay attention to what I'm saying.

PARTNER: Oh, do shut up. Sometimes you can be a real pain.

BULLY: There you are. You're rejecting me.

The Bully's unreasonable, accusatory anger produces a confirmation of love (which is ignored) and an attempt to change the subject. The Bully experiences this latter as a rejection and gets even more offensive. The partner eventually retaliates and what the Bully expected has come about: rejection.

The Clinger cycle

CLINGER: Can't we spend more time together? We're never together enough.

PARTNER: We're hardly ever apart. I love you, but it's just that I do need some space for myself sometimes.

CLINGER: No, no, please don't go now. Stay tonight and go tomorrow.

PARTNER: Look, I really have got to get up early tomorrow, and I could do with a quiet evening on my own.

CLINGER: Please, please, don't go. Don't go. Please.

PARTNER: I can't cope with this. It's too much. I've got to go *now*.

The Clinger wants to be so close that his or her demands create claustrophobia. When the partner protests, this only makes the Clinger more anxious, and he or she clings harder. The partner wriggles more vigorously. The Clinger's grip tightens. Eventually what the Clinger expected happens: abandonment.

Unless these tendencies are very pronounced, they are not usually very obvious right at the start of a relationship. It's only when the attachment bond is solidifying that the difficulties start. However, everyone has insecure tendencies, and these emerge at times of stress in all relationships. A tension-inducing incompatibility on the dominance dimension will stimulate insecurity, as will infidelity caused primarily by splitting or donating on the lust dimension. Either way, all relationships collapse into Bully and Clinger cycles when they begin to go to pieces.

One or other partner then seeks a third party or becomes open to advances as a way of getting out of the cycle. Perhaps the Bully avenges an imagined slight by taking a new lover, or the partner tries to get away from the irrational anger and conflict by having an affair. Perhaps the Clinger is seduced by the possibility of someone safer, or the partner takes a lover to create some distance.

Insecurity produces irrational fears that are a major cause of infidelity.

INCOMPATIBILITY ON THE DOMINANCE DIMENSION

We come now to the last major cause of infidelity.

This can be present right from the start, or it can be caused by a change in the personality of one or both of the members of a couple. People do change, after all, and sometimes this leads to what is often called growing apart. It can, of course, lead to people growing closer as well, but here we are concerned with the causes of infidelity and, therefore, with incompatibility in three respects: clashes in style of aggression, of values and of sexual identity. Let's look at what happens when two people with an SPT on the dominance dimension get together. There are four possible permutations: Wimp–Cosmo, Wimp–Little Princess, Big Boy–Cosmo and Big Boy–Little Princess.

Clashes in style of aggression

You will remember that the Big Boy and Cosmo have an exaggeratedly aggressive style, whereas that of the Wimp and the Little Princess is more concealed and suppressed. This does not mean that the Big Boy and Cosmo or the Wimp and

Little Princess never pair up together. On the contrary, they may enjoy this similarity and find it stimulating – at first, that is. For, if neither changes, sooner or later there are problems.

Big Boy–Cosmo couples

The Big Boy likes to feel he is getting his way; so does Cosmo woman. Neither uses terribly subtle methods of going about getting it. Head-on collisions are inevitable. After the first one no doubt they can make it up, but it leaves a scar, and when another major disagreement comes along the chances are that resentments have been building up that can be dated back to that first clash. If one partner submitted on that occasion, he or she points this out indignantly and effectively insists, 'It's *my* turn to get *my* way. For days [or weeks or even months] I've been compromising.' Perhaps the partner reluctantly gives in as a result, but the cycle only starts again.

On the other hand, perhaps they both compromise from the start. As the first blooms of love begin to fade, it becomes a bigger and bigger strain. Both feel that they never get to do what they really want; it's always some half-measure. They see films neither wanted to see; they go to pubs or restaurants of neither's choosing; they may even have a kind of sexual intercourse that is not fully satisfying to either. Whether in bed or at large, they are not being fulfilled, and in the end furious disputes build up and explode in the open.

If neither changes, they will eventually become an unhappy couple, and the danger of infidelity will be great. At this point their tendencies on the insecurity dimension can exacerbate the problem: if both are bullies, the rows will be even worse. Likewise if one has a strong Splitter or Donor tendency, the danger of an affair increases.

However, it is always possible that one of them will become less dominant under the pressure and that this will suit them. A Cosmo, for example – either because her career is going well and she feels more self-confident as a result or perhaps through deciding to become a mother – may not feel such a strong urge to assert herself in a forthright style. She may become more of a Little Princess, and this may suit the couple better. Likewise a Big Boy may begin to learn that his aggressiveness gets him into unnecessary conflicts both at work and play and, as he gets older, start to tone it down a bit and become more of a Wimp in style. In such circumstances, the couple would be under less strain, and their tendencies on the insecurity and lust dimensions would be less likely to destabilize them and create a climate for infidelity.

Overall, then, this is an incompatible couple whose aggressive styles make them liable to come unstuck unless one undergoes a change in approach.

Wimp–Little Princess couples

Again, since they share a similar style of aggression, these two types may find this fact attractive initially. However, their diffidence, and the covert means by which they try to get their way, leads to trouble.

This is the couple who never seem to be able to make up their minds what to do. Both say, 'I don't mind. You decide,' with the result that to begin with they may end up doing nothing. After a bit they may learn to manipulate each other better, but the resultant politics makes for complexity. They spend so much time using devious tricks to outwit each other that they are liable to forget what they wanted in the first place. Like the Big Boy–Cosmo couple, they are liable to finish up with a compromise that entails doing the things that neither hoped for.

Alternatively, one of them may begin to fill the vacuum by becoming assertive. The Wimp may surprise himself by becoming more of a Big Boy, and this will please the Little Princess, who likes an assertive, aggressive man. Or hitherto unexplored reserves of Cosmo-style dominance may emerge and the Little Princess may step forward – to the Wimp's delight.

But if neither starts wearing the trousers and gets into the driving seat, this will be a directionless, unfulfilled couple that is very vulnerable to a dominant third party: a Big Boy or a Cosmo.

Big Boy–Little Princess couples

This should work fine. The manly displays of confident decision-making and the assertiveness of the Big Boy make him feel in control, and the Little Princess is happy to be able to leave the small things to him while privately feeling that she is the one who really dictates what happens. Her round-about style complements his explicitly aggressive stance. Shifts in personality by either party only give rise to the problems listed above – except, that is, if both shift, in which case they become one of the . . .

Wimp–Cosmo couples

The Wimp finds the Cosmo's style of dominance a relief – it spares him all that macho posing and all those tiresome decisions about where to eat and drink. And for the Cosmo it's nice to find a man who doesn't feel he's got to walk all over her to prove he is one and who actually listens to what she says. So they get along well, with few major disagreements and tiring rows. Shifts in personality, unless these affect both of them, only cause trouble.

Clashes in values

The Wimp's and Cosmo's individualistic, up-front, rebellious philosophy contrasts with the belief in group values, discretion and conformity of the Big Boy and the Little Princess. So long as these are the couplings, they see eye to eye, but cross a Big Boy with a Cosmo or a Wimp with a Little Princess and the arguments begin.

Big Boy–Cosmo couples

During the honeymoon period of the romance each regards the other's values and philosophy as lovable eccentricities. But not for long: 'I just can't believe what you're saying,' You can't really mean *that*,' soon become 'You're so illogical, it's incredible. Can't you see how absurd what you're saying is?' which becomes 'I don't even want to hear what you think, you're such an idiot.'

For the Cosmo it's a constant struggle to get him to take her seriously. For the Big Boy it's her illogicality that sticks in his craw – why doesn't she just stick to talking about the things she understands? Then there's the not so little things, like her insistence that he does his bit of the housework or his dismay at not being cooked for on a regular basis. And if they have children, does he expect her to give up work for five years? Yes, he does.

On a wide variety of issues, from how they should run their life together to how the country should be run, there is unceasing conflict, which no amount of reconciliation can put an end to. Their tendencies on the insecurity dimension are aroused: it's hardly surprising if either feels in danger of being abandoned or feels rejected. Both are highly likely when the right Little Princess (who will look after him 'properly') or the right Wimp (who won't behave like an MCP) comes along. The one who starts the affair will be the one with the Splitter tendency.

Of course, it is always possible that one or both of them will shift their values, he towards a more tolerant view of her desire to do what she wants when she wants, she towards a more traditional, female set of homemaking values. If so, the trouble will correspondingly reduce, but unless the shift is considerable and lasting, the danger of a flare-up of the old differences will be there waiting to be provoked by a calculating third party who wants to sow dissension between them.

Wimp–Little Princess couples

The Wimp can be very vague about things like traffic laws, and he can get steamed up about the way the police behave or the incompetence of the government. While the Little Princess doesn't agree with him about these things, they don't lead to real trouble because they don't really interest her. The big sticking-points are things connected with lifestyle and his career. She likes to keep up appearances in the home, particularly when there are guests, whereas he tends to be very easygoing as a host. He may say things she finds embarrassing or tactless, and she is furious afterwards (she doesn't make a scene in front of the visitors). Likewise she likes to eat out in 'nice' (preferably smart) places; he's equally happy with a take-away. He may say she's a snob because there are signs that she wants to better herself or both of them, and she may say he's a slob. That argument often leads on to one about his career. Why isn't he more ambitious? Why doesn't he ask for a pay rise? Doesn't he care? The answer is that he's quite happy doing what he's doing, and he's not going to waste his time sucking up to the boss. He'd rather not have all that trouble.

If they get married, there are two main dangers: either she drives him towards someone whose values are more like his (a Cosmo) or, even more probable, his lack of get up and go (as she might put it) will mean eventually that she'll look out for someone else – a Big Boy. If she has pronounced Splitter tendencies, and if a snatching Big Boy turns up, a triangle is extremely probable.

On the whole, because neither presses his or her values very strongly (being unaggressive), Wimps and Little Princesses rarely change each other's values, so shifts are rare.

Big Boy–Little Princess couples

They see eye to eye. Problems arise only if she starts reading feminist books and magazines and ramming them down his throat, or if he starts telling her that she should broaden her interests. This sometimes happens when some other aspect of the relationship is not working; then values are used as a way of getting at each other. Strong Bully tendencies in either party can also lead to these changes as a way of attacking the partner.

Wimp–Cosmo couples

Again they agree. However, if the Cosmo starts longing for a stronger man who will look after her, or if the Wimp begins to feel that her independence is a threat, then these changes may be expressed in clashes over values and lifestyle. Here it is likely to be Clinger tendencies that give rise to the problems – either one may express a wish for more security and attention indirectly by attacking the individualistic, independent values of the partner.

Clashes in sexual identity

The Wimp's and the Cosmo's renunciation of sexual stereotypes unites them, while the Big Boy and Little Princess are attracted to each other's more conventional approach to their sexual identities. Crossing the types is highly unproductive!

Big Boy–Cosmo couples

He likes to be on top. To her, variety is the spice of sex. At first she may not mind his missionary zeal in bed, but eventually, when she starts trying to get him to try other possibilities, either he refuses or he doesn't enjoy what happens.

Even before they get into bed there are potential problems. To begin with, she may not mind his conventionally male behaviour – the little courtesies, paying for evenings out and so on – and he may interpret her independence of deed and word as acceptable manifestations of the modern woman. She doesn't much like his classically male style of dressing and he would like to see her in a skirt – a miniskirt, preferably – just a bit more often. But both let these things pass. Eventually, they become irritants, however, and symbols of the partners' different approach to sex. In the end there is a grave danger that she will find herself saying he is immature and crass in his style and his sexual behaviour, and he will accuse her of not really being a woman (possibly even to the point of suggesting that she really prefers her own sex).

So the incompatibility of these types as regards sexual

identity is considerable, and since their life is very likely to go to pieces rapidly, both will probably feel frustrated and open to the possibility of an affair with a more compatible partner. The individualistic, more ambiguous style of a Wimp, combined with his greater flexibility in bed, will attract the Cosmo, and for the Big Boy the stark contrast between his present partner and a flirtatious, 'feminine' (perhaps miniskirted) Little Princess will seem irresistible. Which one succumbs first depends on who has the greater Splitter tendency.

Shifts in sexual identity are very rare, so this would be an improbable solution to the problem.

Wimp–Little Princess couples

He always finds her sexy but at the same time resents the demand that he should initiate what happens in bed. From her point of view, the relationship has been unsatisfactory from the start. He really doesn't give her what she wants at all – a man who is courteous, forceful and does all the work in bed.

He is vulnerable to a more 'understanding' woman (as he would put it), and she is even more vulnerable to a Big Boy knight in shining armour who comes to sweep her off her feet. By the end she is feeling that he is probably homosexual or bisexual, and he is so fed up with her demanding behaviour that it's a great relief to both of them to finish. Unless he has an unusually large Splitter tendency, it's most likely to be she who starts an affair.

If there is to be a shift in sexual identity – a very rare event – then it is most likely to occur in her. Perhaps she is inspired by books or magazines to become more adventurous and assertive in bed. Wimps hardly ever turn into Big Boys in their sexual lives.

Big Boy–Little Princess couples

Their clothing, manners and approach to sex are matched perfectly. The only problem is that they may start to get bored by the predictability of their sexual techniques. Boredom combined with splitting tendencies on either side are the main dangers and can lead to flings with a third party; paradoxically, these flings may eventually rejuvenate their own sex life together. Such cases are rare examples of a triangle that may actually strengthen the original couple.

Wimp–Cosmo couples

Predictability in style or in bed is not a problem for these two. On the contrary, the danger is that they are too keen on variation – to the extent of wanting to experiment with third parties. Both are probably committed to the idea of fidelity, but the problem, at least until they are into their thirties, is that their belief in being individualistic and free can lead to affairs that destabilize the relationship.

LEAGUE TABLE OF COUPLES' VULNERABILITY TO INFIDELITY

Rank	Sexual personality type	Estimated proportion of couples in which infidelity occurs
1.	Donor and Splitter	98%
2.	Bully and Bully	96%
3.	Bully and Cosmo	94%
4.	Splitter and Clinger	92%
5.	Bully and Big Boy	80%
6.	Splitter and Wimp	75%
7.	Splitter and Cosmo	75%
8.	Bully and Donor	74%
9.	Splitter and Little Princess	72%
10.	Splitter and Big Boy	72%
11.	Donor and Cosmo	68%
12.	Donor and Big Boy	68%
13.	Big Boy and Cosmo	67%
14.	Donor and Wimp	66%

Rank	Sexual personality type	Estimated proportion of couples in which infidelity occurs
15.	Clinger and Little Princess	65%
16.	Donor and Little Princess	60%
17.	Clinger and Wimp	60%
18.	Wimp and Little Princess	58%
19.	Splitter and Bully	58%
20.	Clinger and Clinger	52%
21.	Bully and Wimp	50%
22.	Bully and Little Princess	50%
23.	Clinger and Donor	46%
24.	Clinger and Bully	45%
25.	Clinger and Cosmo	45%
26.	Clinger and Big Boy	45%
27.	Big Boy and Little Princess	35%
28.	Wimp and Cosmo	35%

7 THE TWENTY-EIGHT TYPES OF COUPLE

DONOR AND SPLITTER

Position in league: **First**
Estimated proportion of this type of couple that has
   affairs: **98%**
Most likely unfaithful: **Splitter**
Most likely third party: **Snatcher**

Case history

Gerry, the faithful Donor
Diane, the unfaithful Splitter
A variety of third parties

Diane is now in her mid-forties, but in over twenty years of married life she's lost count of the number of affairs she's had. She thinks the very first one after the wedding was the most significant. 'I'd always liked being sexy, you know, and at school I managed to have a great time – without everyone knowing or being called a slag. I was careful about where and when and who found out about it – I didn't brag. After I left school I started going steady and being more settled, but it didn't stop me having the odd fling – which meant that when I finally decided to marry Gerry I was only fooling myself when I told myself I'd give up the little thrills on the side. But I believed it at the time. It lasted about nine months, I think. For one thing, Gerry had always been a bit predictable between the sheets. I like variety, and he doesn't really understand about that.

'My vow of fidelity came a cropper after about nine months when I met Dean. He arrived in the packing department at work and started giving me the eye. Since I'd been married I'd usually flirted, but that was all. Anyway, when he came into our local a few evenings later – it turned out he lived nearby – we got talking. Gerry didn't seem to mind, and I even introduced them.

'At work I kept Dean at bay and he played it cool until one day I was down in packing with a message, and he suddenly put his hand on my cheek and stroked it.

'Since then I've had a lot of affairs. I love Gerry, but it's no good pretending: I'm just not the faithful type. Thank God, Gerry understands my needs and doesn't make a fuss. And I'm careful because what the eye doesn't see . . .'

Gerry says: 'Of course, I knew Diane had flings before we married. She even told me about them, and we used to laugh about them because they didn't make me jealous – we were always on–off at that time. I used to think it was quite funny.

'When we married she swore she'd give it all up. Well, she did, until after about three years of marriage, when I think she was feeling a bit bored. At the time I probably wasn't giving her all the attention she deserved, and I caught her at it one day when I came home from work during the day. Of course, I was furious. But now I've learnt to accept it. It's what she's like, and you can't change people, can you? I mean, sex isn't the only thing in a relationship, and she doesn't do it very often. And she *is* a very fine-looking woman, so I haven't got much choice. I can't help it if men find my wife irresistible. I've tried everything to stop her, but it's inevitable. People say it's natural for men to want to stray but that's rubbish. Women have their urges too, you know. I don't like it but it's only happened a few times, and life's all about compromises, isn't it?'

Regarding the types of Third Party, they have been various. Diane wants variety above all things and she has tried most of them with men of all kinds.

Profile

Not surprisingly, if people whose desire wanes when they get familiar with a lover, and who start fancying other people as a result, pair up with partners who expect (and even want) their lover to have affairs, then affairs is what they get. The result may be an 'open' relationship in which the Splitter is granted a great deal of licence. In these cases, or even when the agreement is not explicit, affairs don't shake this relationship as much as they would disturb more exclusive, monogamous ones.

However they describe it to themselves, the Donor and the Splitter almost invariably enter a cycle:

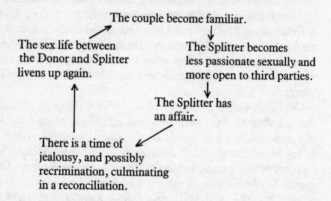

The couple become familiar.

The Splitter becomes less passionate sexually and more open to third parties.

The Splitter has an affair.

There is a time of jealousy, and possibly recrimination, culminating in a reconciliation.

The sex life between the Donor and Splitter livens up again.

A Donor–Splitter couple in which the Splitter has no affairs is extremely rare indeed. Take the most stable coupling possible:

	Partner 1	Partner 2
Sexual personality type	Donor	Splitter
Second tendency	Cosmo	Wimp
Third tendency	Bully	Clinger

The compatibility on the Dominance dimension brings them close together, and when instability arises a Bully–Clinger combination is the least unstable. Yet getting on well is in itself a problem for a couple with these SPTs: it is being close that causes the infidelity! Closeness means familiarity, and that means the Splitter goes off sex and starts to roam, while the uneasy Donor supports this behaviour, believing there must be a better lover for his or her partner. If they love each other, their sex life becomes very dead: it's when they feel unfamiliar that things click in bed. So it's only in very exceptional circumstances that compatibility leads to fidelity: out of an intense love for their partners Splitters forgo sex altogether, preferring to avoid affairs and have an impoverished sex life; that way they avoid the affairs which set off the Donor–Splitter cycle and all the anguish those usually entail. But even this does not make Donors any happier; their guilt is inflamed by having their partner all to themselves. Finally, a Clinger third tendency makes the Splitter that little bit less likely to have affairs: Clingers are always nervous unfaithfuls.

The worst combination for this couple normally results in not only affairs but divorce:

	Partner 1	Partner 2
Sexual personality type	Donor	Splitter
Second tendency	Bully	Bully
Third tendency	Big Boy	Cosmo

The strong Bully tendencies produce awful rows, and at first the Splitter is very liable to use affairs as a means of revenge. After a bit the Splitter realizes that they are an ineffectual weapon to use against a Donor. But then they get along so badly in terms of style of aggression, values and sexual identity that this makes the almost continuous cycle even more destabilizing than usual.

What with the constant infidelity, rows and clashes on the dominance dimension, it's a wonder this combination lasts five minutes. Yet, paradoxically, Donors and Splitters are kept together by the one thing that destroys most relationships: infidelity. The repeated experience of affair-recrimination–reconciliation–better sex–familiarity–affair is craved by this couple. Like agonized addicts, they may battle on for years, the Donor giving away and regaining the partner, the Splitter having affairs and reuniting. Neither is quite able to break the habit.

The Snatcher is the natural companion for the Splitter's affairs. Although the Snatcher will eventually be frustrated by the Splitter's refusal to leave the faithful Donor, at first they are very excited by each other. The frustrated Splitter gets the sexual feast he or she is longing for, and the Snatcher finds an exceptionally willing partner in the triangle game.

BULLY AND BULLY

Position in league: **Second**
Estimated proportion of this type of couple that has
   affairs: **96%**
Most likely unfaithful: **A Bully with a Splitter second
   tendency and a Cosmo/Big Boy third tendency**
Most likely third party: **Wimp or Little Princess**

Case history

Sheila, the faithful Bully
Sean, the unfaithful Bully
Gloria, the third-party Clinger

Two more incompatible and insecure individuals than Sheila and Sean you could hardly hope to meet. Mutual rejection and running sores nursed by resentment characterized their relationship. What kept them going was the making up after the rows. 'Sexual healing', they called it. Gloria was a friend to both of them. As a Clinger she put up with the incessant rat-a-tat-tat of their public disharmony, for they made very unrewarding company on a night out. It was only in private, in bed, that a synchrony was to be found. In between times, they'd be threatening each other, a highly unstable human concoction.

There came a Sunday when Sean felt Sheila had gone too far. She chucked the lunch he had carefully prepared into the cat dish and flounced out of the house. At a loss for someone on whom to work off his anger at this rejection, he found himself wandering round to see if Gloria was in. She was. Sunbathing in the garden. He sat raging for a time in the sun, then he burst into tears. She put her arms around him, perfectly aware of what might happen. It did.

Within two and a half weeks it was all over between Sean and Sheila. Gloria came as a tremendous relief, with her clinging preparedness to listen and calm him down. It is often the way where two Bullies are together: the one who has a greater Splitter tendency leaves for a Clinger.

Profile

An explosive combination, liable to ignite at any time. Both reject, expect to be rejected and get furious when it happens. Infidelity is a very likely method for seeking revenge for a Bully. Third parties can expect to be used as a weapon for attacking the partner. The Bully–Bully couple can be that rare thing, a couple in which both partners set up triangles.

There is some mystery about how these two types come to be together in the first place. They may be attracted by their similarity, initially spending much time talking and coming to feel that they have a special understanding which forms a safe harbour from the hostile, storm-tossed ocean of life. At this point their bullying behaviour may be overlooked or not much in evidence.

Or perhaps they have compatible dominance tendencies. Wimp–Cosmo or Big Boy–Little Princess second tendencies form the basis for shared activities and new-found enjoyment that postpone awareness of the less secure and more unattractive bullying features that each possesses.

Another possibility, albeit rare, is that soon after their affair starts there is a shift towards clinging by one of them.

This can happen when one is significantly more of a Bully than the other and pushes the partner towards a more clinging expression of insecurity. Such a shift is usually accompanied by a dominant second tendency on the part of the very pronounced Bully and submissive tendencies on the other's part.

Whatever the cause of the attraction, this coupling almost invariably gives rise to infidelity and leaves in its wake a pile of mangled third parties. The most vulnerable combination to infidelity is as follows:

	Partner 1	Partner 2
Sexual personality type	Bully	Bully
Second tendency	Splitter	Big Boy/Cosmo
Third tendency	Cosmo/Big Boy	Donor

This combination always leads to infidelity. On top of the Bully rows, there are tremendous battles of will: the Bully with the dominant second tendency makes the Bully with the Splitter second tendency feel doubly determined to damage the partner and show just how little he or she cares. A partner with Donor second tendency and dominant third tendency is not exactly a prescription for fidelity, but it is marginally less vulnerable because it rouses the Splitter Bully's anger less.

The least vulnerable combination is still very vulnerable:

	Partner 1	Partner 2
Sexual personality type	Bully	Bully
Second tendency	Big Boy	Little Princess
Third tendency	Donor	Splitter

While Little Princesses do like their men to be assertive and strong and while they do like being unfaithful as much as their Cosmo sisters (at least when young), they do get very cheesed off if their men are rude, inconsiderate and liable to fly off the handle. If, on top of this, they are Bullies, sooner or later they will use an affair as a means of getting the loving sex they want (their Bully partner's miffs are a turn-off) but, above all, as a clear signal of rejection.

Wimps or Little Princesses are the most likely third parties for this couple. Their laid-back style and preference for dominant partners can lead them to find a Bully attractive (on a good day Bullies can be very charismatic). However, if no submissive type can be persuaded, Clingers are always a possibility, as is the ubiquitous Snatcher who is ever ready to add to the considerable dissension in this couple.

BULLY AND COSMO

Position in league: **Third**
Estimated proportion of this type of couple that has
 affairs: **94%**
Most likely unfaithful: **Cosmo**
Most likely third party: **Wimp**

Case history

Jean, the faithful Cosmo
Richard, the unfaithful Bully
Sue, the third party Little Princess

Richard says: 'Jean would bustle around the place like a manic computer at weekends and in the evenings. She was always being brisk and efficient about knitting a sweater or learning a new language or some other self-improving scheme.'

Jean says: 'Richard just couldn't stand it if I got on with my life. If I was at home, he would try to force me to sit down with him to watch telly or, more likely, for some snogging. Well, there's more to life. It used to really piss me off when he complained that I went out to evening classes. I'm a free agent.'

The Bully/Big Boy wants to dominate 'his girl'. The Cosmo wants to be called a 'woman' and she isn't his or anybody else's.

Richard goes on: 'And she used to drag me round those bloody stately home places. All I wanted to do was to settle down for a good tea if we had to go, but by the time we'd gone round all those rooms full of clapped-out relics she'd want to go for "a nice healthy walk". You must be kidding. Stay in the tea-room till the pubs open – that was my line.'

Jean's job took her away for long periods. When Richard's friend Tim stopped going out with Sue, Richard gave Sue a ring to see if she was all right because they'd always been quite friendly. Regular meetings ensued. From his point of view, she was a far better partner; Sue was on the rebound and found Richard by no means unsuitable. Gradually but inexorably he preferred Sue to Jean, whose attitude to the whole thing was: 'If that's what you want, you're a free agent. I'm not your mother.' Actually, Jean was hurt by the affair and upset that a Little Princess like Sue had got her man. Eventually, once she had admitted this to herself, she was able to realize that she would be much happier without Richard anyway. Leaving aside Sue (who would be better off with a Big Boy), it was for the best.

Profile

How did the Cosmo make the mistake of getting involved with a Bully? Perhaps she just ignored the signals of brash aggro because he had something that distracted her – wealth, charm or looks. Or maybe she latched on to a minor characteristic that made him seem 'special'. Or again the courting stage may have gone so smoothly that his bullying only came out later. Whatever the reason, she's made a mistake.

And so has he. Her assertive and independent style only serves to worsen his insecurities. Though he gets angry and defensive when confronted by it, he's really shrinking with trepidation. Rejection seems just around the corner regardless of what she says. She's out late one night (later than he expected) with an old girlfriend; she doesn't call one weekend when she's staying with her parents. Any of these sorts of occurrence throw him into a rage, and she is not at all pleased by his reaction. She experiences it as male possessiveness when, in truth, it's blind terror.

If he's prone to sexual jealousy, it can end in violence. There is a psychiatric condition called 'conjugal jealousy'; some Bully types invent fictional affairs on the part of their partners and ignore all evidence to the contrary. (Perhaps one quarter of all domestic murders each year have this cause.) So if you're a Cosmo, it's terribly important to pay attention if, in the early stages of a relationship, your man shows bullying tendencies. Getting it wrong could prove fatal!

Even at its most compatible this couple rarely works:

	Partner 1	Partner 2
Sexual personality type	Bully	Cosmo
Second tendency	Wimp	Clinger
Third tendency	Splitter	Donor

The mitigating factor is obviously the Wimpish second tendency that attracts the Cosmo but is confusing to her too. She is puzzled by the conflict between her loving feelings towards his low-key Wimp side and the eruptions of bullying that outrage her. He just seems so contradictory.

Deep down, the Wimp in this Bully *knows* his bullying destroys their intimacy and love, yet he feels powerless to prevent it. He's lying there in bed with her, feeling secure and sexually satisfied, and then she says she's got to be away from him. Suddenly he hears himself attacking her. It's as if he's a man possessed.

Over the years the chances are that this tendency will clash too often. There'll be too many scars for it to last.

The most vulnerable combination is:

	Partner 1	Partner 2
Sexual personality type	Bully	Cosmo
Second tendency	Big Boy	Bully
Third tendency	Donor	Splitter

This combination is rare because in most cases the minute these two types are introduced they take an instant dislike to each other. Normally, a fight for dominance precludes any sort of loving relationship. However, a number of factors can, exceptionally, bring them together.

Competitiveness may cause them to start using sex as a weapon in their war. Maybe she seduces him just to show him who's boss. Or maybe both have a sado-masochistic streak that sucks them into a cycle of hurting each other. Or maybe it's the attraction of similarity, born of narcissism – they want a lifelong affair with themselves. Another variation is if the Cosmo is on the rebound and feeling vulnerable, yet filled with a desire for revenge. She may act the Little Princess at first – appealing to his Big Boy side – and then hit him where it hurts, at the most painful moment, as a displaced revenge on men in general and her last boyfriend in particular.

In most cases it is the Cosmos who will be the unfaithful partner. Only when the Bully is also a Big Boy is he likely to be the one to use infidelity as the way out – with the kind of Little Princess that pisses off his Cosmo partner and gives him what he really wants.

Not even very deep down, a Cosmo does not want a Bully for a partner. Sooner rather than later, she will begin to find more Wimpish and clinging types attractive. When her dream Wimp walks into her life – at work, at supper, in a bus queue, anywhere – she will instantly realize that she has made a mistake. Only if she's locked into caring for her Bully or a sado-masochistic war will she hesitate before either leaving him outright or embarking on a brief affair that ends the same way.

SPLITTER AND CLINGER

Position in league: **Fourth**
Estimated proportion of this type of couple that has
   affairs: **92%**
Most likely unfaithful: **Splitter**
Most likely third party: **Snatcher**

Case history

Betty, the faithful Clinger
Mick, the unfaithful Splitter
Gemma, the third-party Snatcher

Betty has long, thin legs. Miniskirts were made for her. At 25 her skin is clear and smooth, and her pretty snub nose rounds off an impression of great natural desirability. Aged 30, Mick is good-looking in his own way too, solidly built with a square, honest face. Why he should have any wish to chase other women is wholly incomprehensible to their friends.

Mick says: 'Strangely enough, I never screwed around much when I was young. But then I met Betty. She was the most beautiful girl I'd ever slept with. It was like an addiction for me to see her naked. I could happily just look at her or stroke her. And it was love, really, as well. She was very warm and friendly and all that.

'After we married I began to find her a bit too loving. Once I was at an away match with the lads and we didn't get back until much later than I'd told her. She was hysterical when I got in. She seemed to want to be with me all the time and she became like "the wife", you know. She's not adventurous. She's vulnerable and like a nervy kid, really.

'Gemma's not like that at all. I can never get hold of her when I want to, and she's always unpredictable in bed. Gemma's not as "pretty" as Betty, but she's twice as sexy, to my way of thinking. I can't possess her, whereas Betty's like a doormat. I don't honestly believe it hurts Betty so long as she doesn't find out.'

Betty: 'I would be shattered if I thought he might go off with another woman. He's such a lovely man, and it was so romantic when we first started going out. Even now, after all this time, I still long to be with Mick and I get terrified at the idea that anything could happen to him. I once saw him talking to a woman in the pub, and I told him I'd kill myself if he went off with someone else. He understands that, and I believe in him. I don't want anyone else.'

Gemma: 'Mick is a challenge. There he is, with that stunning wife, and yet he wants me. I like Mick. He's a good bloke. But I don't see anything long-term developing. We've both got our partners, and it's best to keep it this way. I've met Betty socially a bit, and I wouldn't want to hurt her. Sometimes I can't help laughing to myself that Mick fancies me more than her.'

Profile

This is your classic roving Jack the Lad, whose partner is a doormat and puts up with affair after affair. In recent years such partners have probably increased considerably in number; long-suffering clinging is a consequence of what some people refer to as the 'New Man' – also on the up. As a couple they can occasionally get along fine, especially where the Clinger's second tendency is Donor. In this case, a roving partner actually suits his or her basic temperament, and even the Clinger needn't feel abandoned so long as the Splitter achieves the desired goal in a way that doesn't threaten total loss of love and accessibility. So long as the Clinger doesn't get wind of it, there's no problem because your Clinger (unlike the Bully) isn't looking to sniff out affairs in a partner.

However, more common is a chain that goes:

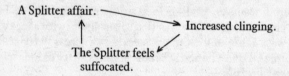

This can go on over a period of weeks, months or years. The Splitter's feeling of suffocation may build up slowly or rapidly, but, either way, the tighter the clinging, the more the Splitter seeks a way out through sex elsewhere: the Clinger's very reaction brings about precisely what it is intended to avoid.

This couple is one of the few that often has its best chance of survival if the Splitter continues to have affairs. With other kinds of partner, this would lead in the end to the collapse of the relationship, but with the right kind of Clinger partner, it can survive affairs. The most vulnerable combination is:

	Partner 1	Partner 2
Sexual personality type	Splitter	Clinger
Second tendency	Big Boy	Donor
Third tendency	Bully	Cosmo

The Clinger's Donor tendency encourages the splitting, but problems on the dominance dimension may be at least as important. Clashes between the Big Boy–Cosmo values, style of aggression and so forth upset this couple's stability and create longstanding bones of contention. The Big Boy gets more and more indignant at the Cosmo's clinging demands, and they seem epitomized by her Cosmo-ness. The Cosmo fuels the fire. Sooner or later a Snatcher Little Princess cleans up. Something similar happens when the Splitter is female and a Cosmo.

Where the Splitter is a Wimp or Little Princess, the speed of break-up may be slower but equally likely in the long run. These types are less prone to boat-rocking, but they will find the clinging distasteful – there is no sign of the forceful assertiveness they look for in a partner. Whatever the permutation, this couple is very liable to have a sex life that breaks down because the Splitter goes off the Clinger.

On the whole, they part as friends unless the Bully is very pronounced in the Splitter or the Clinger becomes so panic-stricken that bad feeling results. *In extremis*, the Clinger may hang around the Splitter's home after the separation or persist in finding out where the ex-partner is socializing, to everyone's embarrassment.

The least vulnerable combination is:

	Partner 1	Partner 2
Sexual personality type	Splitter	Clinger
Second tendency	Compatibility on the dominance dimension	
Third tendency	Clinger	Donor

Either the compatibility on the dominance dimension (Big Boy–Little Princess or Wimp–Cosmo combinations) unites with the Splitter's need to cling to overcome the desire to be unfaithful, or occasional infidelity is offset by the overall satisfaction provided by the relationship.

When infidelity has become an accepted part of the *status quo* it must be handled tactfully by the Splitter. However much of a clinger a Little Princess may be, she will not put up with public humiliation. And if the Splitter is a Cosmo, she must not be made to feel that her partner is scoring points through his affairs.

Little Princesses in this position may try to justify their partner's peccadillos by saying that men have urges and there's no point trying to ignore them. The Cosmo will adopt a different tack: 'He leads his life. I lead mine. What counts is the relationship, and so long as he doesn't damage that, we lead our separate lives.'

When the Splitters are male, pride may make the situation of having an unfaithful partner more difficult. Vestiges of the idea that a man should be boss will particularly trouble Big Boy Clingers. It is less likely that this arrangement will survive in such cases. Wimps have less ego about such matters, and the relationship will stand a better chance. But there's a limit to how far they can be pushed – as with Little Princesses.

Given the least vulnerable combination, a Snatcher third party may find it uphill work to prise a Splitter away if he or she has settled into a largely asexual pattern. It's too painful for the Splitter to awaken desire again. If the Splitter has taken to substitute fantasizing, the Snatcher has got to find a way to get the nascent Splitter to connect his or her fantasies with a real, red-hot opportunity. However, when a Splitter–Clinger couple are incompatible on the dominance dimension a Snatcher who is compatible with the Splitter will have a field day.

BULLY AND BIG BOY

Position in league: **Fifth**
Estimated proportion of this type of couple that has
   affairs: **80%**
Most likely unfaithful: **Big Boy**
Most likely third party: **Little Princess**

Case history

John, the faithful Big Boy
Julia, the unfaithful Bully
Simon, the third-party Wimp

Julia often shouted at John, even for doing things that he hadn't contemplated doing. She found him patronizing when he was only trying to help: 'Look, Julia, it's simple enough. Drop the car off after you've gone to the hairdresser's, and why not shop for those clothes you want while you're waiting for the garage to fix it?'

She would shout back: 'Don't tell me what to do! I can run my own life. You look after yours, and I'll look after mine. Just bloody well leave it to me what I do, all right?'

Well, John didn't want his 'little pussycat' screaming at him, and he would get angry too. On the subject of the futility of politicians, for example, he felt he was an expert, yet she would insist on knowing better and ramming her belief in 'total commitment' down his throat. It hurt his male pride to be bullied on his pet subjects.

The rows were awesome to behold.

Julia's bullying side was making her very domineering and, in arguments, very touchy. At the same time her Cosmo second tendency was clashing with John's Big Boy sexual personality type – she felt he was patronizing her because she was female. Only John's Clinger desire to be looked after was keeping them together. She admits now that she was consciously looking for someone and that as soon as she saw Simon – a distant work acquaintance of John – when picking John up from the pub after work one day, she felt something for him. A Wimp with a Snatcher second tendency, Simon wasn't the argumentative type and he fancied her strength and persistence. Much to John's consternation, she made her feelings pretty obvious, and all Simon had to do was to ease things along with the odd look or word or two.

Simon says: 'For about a month things were really good. Then she started trying to redecorate the flat, tell me what new clothes I should buy and so on. It felt more and more as if I were her pet. When John told her it was over, so did I. I thought she'd get over it but I think she still hasn't, two years later.'

Wimps don't like being bullied, and once they've snatched they go off sex. Simon was no exception. Julia was left high and dry. This is all too frequently the outcome for a Bully with Cosmo tendencies who is unfaithful to a Big Boy.

Profile

The Bully's anger and rejection upset the Big Boy. He does not like his woman to shout at him. It makes him doubt her sanity at times and, at others, wish she would drop dead.

Why he's with her is a bit of a mystery. Perhaps he has clinging tendencies and wants to be bullied to some extent – wants to be ruled. Perhaps she's a sex bomb and this has blinded him to her incompatibility. Perhaps she's rich or the centre of attention and attraction in their circle. Whatever has got him into this mess, it's not long before he's beginning to regret it.

For her it's an agonizing race against time to see if she can stop rocking the boat by her bullying. Deep down, she *knows* her petulant outbursts are irrational and upset him, yet when they are building up she feels unable to control and take charge of herself. She knows he was late for a good reason and yet she can't help taking it personally, knows that his lack of expressiveness tonight is because he's just finished a three-day work binge and is tired out, and yet she hears herself starting up shrill, whingeing remonstrations regardless: 'Oh, yes, I know the traffic was bad, but *you could have phoned.*' (No, he couldn't.) 'You're so unaffectionate. You're so cold. Why can't you just be nice to me once in a while? *I'm sick of being ignored.*' (Mostly he doesn't do anything of the sort.)

However, this basic picture can be modified by the personality types. At its least vulnerable the combination is:

	Partner 1	Partner 2
Sexual personality type	Bully	Big Boy
Second tendency	Little Princess	Clinger
Third tendency	Splitter	Donor

Her very contrariness may itself attract him: one minute she's a raging bull; the next she's his Little Princess. If he does get fed up, his lack of Splitter tendencies means that he's unlikely to console himself by an affair. In this version she's the more likely to do this – probably after a row, and the worse for drink, she may hop into bed with a Big Boy friend who's played his cards right. But this would be rarer than her accusing her regular partner of infidelity – something Bullies are prone to.

At its most vulnerable this couple doesn't stand a chance:

	Partner 1	Partner 2
Sexual personality type	Bully	Big Boy
Second tendency	Cosmo	Splitter
Third tendency	Donor	Bully

What brings this combination together is always a mystery to their friends. Talk of 'chemistry' and 'something intangible' is often heard when they try to explain it. Usually it's something pretty simple: a shared love of the sado-masochistic enjoyment of inflicting and receiving pain; wealth, status, power or all three in both partners; a tactical union, to do with work; a delusion that each has discovered a double – they see themselves when looking at each other.

From day one it's stormy. Before long the sex has become torture. She only wants it when he doesn't and vice versa. What may have started as exciting rough stuff degenerates into a way of getting at each other.

It's the Big Boy who looks elsewhere, with a lustful longing for quieter, jollier, 'feminine' Little Princesses who are often a good deal younger than the current partner and a lot less grief. He lies in late with his mistress, wondering how he can face going back to his Bully–Cosmo and how he could have ever got involved with her.

The break-up is bloody and hideous for mutual friends to behold. The Cosmo may make it into a *cause célèbre* of women's rights, may accuse him of abusing her and of betrayal. If there is some practical means of putting the boot in, she will. If they work together, he'd better watch out for mysterious problems at the office – bad-mouthing and suddenly getting cut by previously friendly acquaintances. It's all very nasty and, worst of all, she just won't leave it alone. His Big Boy notions of gentlemanly chivalry take a hard battering; with any luck, he learns a few lessons about what sort of woman will suit him. She is liable to learn nothing and to bear a grudge for years afterwards.

The Third Party is invariably a Little Princess, usually clinging. She doesn't need to be a Snatcher because she'll be motivated by pity for him. The affair may start with her offering consolation; suddenly they see the light. For him the nightmare is over. For his ex-partner it has just begun.

SPLITTER AND WIMP

Position in league: **Sixth**
Estimated proportion of this type of couple that has
   affairs: **75%**
Most likely unfaithful: **Splitter**
Most likely third party: **Someone who is compatible with
splitter on dominance dimension**

Case history

Doug, the faithful Wimp
Jeanie, the unfaithful Splitter
Bill, the third-party Big Boy

Jeanie was a big, bouncy Little Princess. At 33 she'd seen
better days, but on a good night she had a lot of charisma. It
troubled Doug that she would tend to get rather drunk on a
good night and be fairly blatant in her interest in other men.
However, he always got her home safely in the end. The real
damage was all done while she was sober – with his Big Boy
best pal, Bill.

Jeanie says: 'Doug and I were well suited: the attraction of
opposites. I could wrap my arms round him and encircle him
in love, and for the first few years that was all that mattered.
What with the kids and my yoga and the childbirth classes
that I teach, I was too busy for anything else. OK, I'd get a bit
tiddly down the pub and sometimes steal a kiss or two, but it
didn't cause any harm. The real trouble started with Bill.'

Bill takes up the story: 'Doug and I went back a long way.
We listened to records together when we were nine, and I got
him out of several scrapes by the canal when we used to have
gang fights. When they got married I wasn't best man
because we'd grown apart a bit at that time. Doug seemed
very happy, and I wished them both well. Then I got this
itch. I began to look for excuses to see Jeanie. I knew it was

wrong and that it would hurt Doug, but I couldn't help feeling I was better suited to her and that nothing could stop us. My chance came when it turned out that her yoga class was just round the corner from where I did my interval training on a Wednesday night. It was only natural to offer her a lift home.

'At first it was all very innocent. She'd forgotten about the pub incident and just thought of me as her husband's best pal. But gradually we felt more and more serious about each other. I could tell she was warming to me but she couldn't admit it to herself. One night, just as an experiment, I pecked her on the cheek when we parted and she blushed. The next time, I pretended to miss her cheek and scored a direct hit on her mouth. Finally, I put an arm on her shoulder and she didn't move it.'

Doug remembers: 'They told me together. It was a big shock. I was enraged, but I was clever: I hid it. I'll never forgive you Bill, you bastard, I thought, but I didn't show it, I knew she was right for me and that it was a temporary thing she'd get over. And what about the kids, eh?

'Well, my plan worked out. I made her feel guilty. I may be a quietish sort of bloke, but nobody steals my woman. I let them carry on because I knew I'd win out in the end. Sure enough, once she'd got him the sex was less exciting: she stopped seeing him nine months ago and I reckon it was a passing phase. My only worry is that something like it will happen again.'

Profile

Although the Splitter is the more likely to roam, the key question here is who is most likely to break the relationship off?

The core lies in the Wimp's response to the Splitter's philandering, and this depends on the personality types of both individuals. At one extreme the Wimp may be reasonably content with a Cosmo Splitter. At the other he will become deeply discontented with a Little Princess or a Bully.

But mostly the Wimp in this couple feels dissatisfied and gets fed up with her incorrigible ways. Your Wimp is a tolerant bloke and more prepared than the next man to see that there are two sides to every argument. But he has his pride, and above all he doesn't usually want a relationship that lurches from one crisis to another. Since crises are meat and drink to the Splitter, there is an inbuilt incompatibility.

At their most vulnerable, they combine as follows:

	Partner 1	Partner 2
Sexual personality type	Splitter	Wimp
Second tendency	Little Princess	Donor
Third tendency	Bully	Bully

Mutual rejection lurks like a thin patch of ice on the surface of this relationship. Wimp and Little Princess skate past each other, somehow never able to hold hands and keep their balance together. They have never really connected properly as a couple, never really understood each other's attitudes or love each other's faults. Their dance can end at any time with a plunge into icy-cold water if they collapse into open hatred and mutual rejection. But at the heart lies the problem of the Little Princess's affairs.

The Wimp may be tolerant at first. It's not in either of their natures to be upfront about things, so he will probably only guess about the affairs – no spontaneous late-night confessions. Once he is sure, he'll probably turn a blind eye or at least prefer not to have a row about it.

But as their sex life wanes things get worse. She wants to be petted and seduced, to feel she's being possessed by a big, strong man. She wants to be conquered. He wants nothing of the sort. He wants the relationship to be more equal than that, to feel he's giving her pleasure as well as getting his own.

This basic sexual incompatibility rapidly becomes intolerable when she starts her affairs. Suddenly he seems repulsive, probably even pathetic, to her. In the end either or both may call it a day: he probably goes off with a Cosmo, she with a Big Boy, although both are highly vulnerable to a well-organized snatch. The parting and aftermath are no bloodbath, though their Bully side creates resentment which appears in round-about ways – she 'forgets' to leave him those keys, and he somehow never gets round to giving her back those videos he accidentally took away with him.

At its least vulnerable this combination can work well:

	Partner 1	Partner 2
Sexual personality type	Splitter	Wimp
Second tendency	Cosmo	Clinger
Third tendency	Clinger	Donor

Glued together by that powerful bond which always goes with a Clinger–Clinger combination, and on the same wavelength regarding dominance, the only fly in the ointment is her splitting.

If she's sensible in her choice of lovers and diplomatic about them, he may never find out. Wimp–Clingers aren't suspicious types, so if she has quiet affairs with low-key lovers the inevitable periodic lack of sexual interest on her part can seem insignificant to him.

If, however, she insists on making a big deal out of her infidelity and incorporates it into the relationship as evidence of her independence and right to lead her own life, there will be trouble. Unless he's a raving Clinger, he's going to feel injured and question the whole situation. At first he may be tolerant, but there's a limit to how far he'll let the ideology and talk of women's rights distract him from a basic feeling of unease. After all, not only is he not getting much sex, but he's also having to put up with a good deal of disruption and uncertainty because the Clinger in him is bound to worry that she'll go off with one of her lovers.

So in this variation it may well be he, not she, who finally, after a great deal of heart-searching, feels that it's no longer any use trying to keep it going. But it may take many years before he gets to that point because much unites them, and the Clinger in him is against bust-ups and change.

If he does go off with another woman, it's almost certain to be a Cosmo with a Clinger or Snatcher second tendency. For her it could be a wily Snatcher who's determined not to take second place to a Wimp. He may be a Big Boy who manages to conceal his less attractive side until he's achieved his goal. For a woman with a Cosmo tendency the Big Boy can be quite appealing as a contrast to the Wimp in this scenario.

SPLITTER AND COSMO

Position in league: **Seventh**
Estimated proportion of this type of couple that has
    affairs: **75%**
Most likely unfaithful: **Splitter**
Most likely third party: **Someone who is compatible with Splitter on dominance dimension**

Case history

Sally, the faithful Cosmo
Tim, the unfaithful Splitter
Georgina, the third-party Little Princess

Tim had had affairs since about three years after they'd married. Sally probably knew about them deep down in her heart of hearts but couldn't admit it. Georgina was different from all the others because Tim felt a kind of reverence for her; she was a Little Princess from a higher social class than either his or Sally's. Affairs that cross class barriers have a huge impact on all concerned, and this case was no exception.

Tim says: 'Sally can provide most of what I want from a woman. She's warm and confident, and above all she knows her own mind. If we're in France on a camping holiday and I can't decide where to pitch the tent and it's late and the kids are screaming, she's brilliant. She'll just take over and sort everything out.

'But I don't believe one woman can supply all your needs. Sally is fine, but she can be very crass and obvious. And the rows are terrible if she's being obstinate. What was missing from my life was sophistication, subtlety, a person who could relate to the more refined parts of me, deep down. Georgina fulfilled that need. She was gentle, soft and cultivated. A bit of a Sloane Ranger but all the nicer for it. She could pay her own way, although I never let her.

'I first went to her flat about an insurance claim. She'd been in Turkey on holiday and had some cameras stolen. It was my job to check that the claim was legitimate. That first time she made a big impression on me. She was educated and amusing and a real contrast to most of the women I'd met before. I made an excuse to see her again about the claim, and at the end of the next visit I chanced my arm and asked her out to dinner. I had to fork out quite a bit of cash on two more dinners before I got my first real kiss, but it was so different from Sally – when we were courting she always insisted on paying her share. It was great to be able to treat Georgy like a lady, to pander to her.

'That first kiss was a big event because it meant she'd made up her mind in spite of the fifteen-year difference in our ages.'

Georgina says: 'The thing is, he made me laugh a lot. He may not have been my age, and he was a bit uncertain about things – the first time he took me out to dinner we went to an *awful* place – but he made a big effort to find out what I liked. Instead of taking me for granted like the boys who normally take me out, he was actually making an effort to be nice. And he was serious and persistent.

'I guessed he was married, which to me was an insurance policy because I knew it couldn't last. But I never challenged him about it. You see, I know I'm not all that brilliant-looking, and it was just super to be cosseted for once. I was fed up with having to play the modern woman. Of course, it's not a long-term thing, and the trouble would be if he started getting heavy. But I think he knows the situation and won't push it.'

Profile

Your liberated Cosmo may think, intellectually, that if a partner wants to have an affair, she should not stand in his way. On an emotional plane things are usually very different. The way this couple develops depends largely on how she deals with these conflicting factors. In most cases her heart will eventually rule her head but not without a great deal of talking and thinking and agonizing.

The Splitter in this couple has to be very careful not to make her feel that he's putting one over her through his affairs. The moment she feels that they in any way are a matter of competition or exploitation, he's in trouble. He must also be clever in the way he encourages or discourages her perception of his affairs: if he lets her heart take over from her ideas about freedom and independence, she'll show him the door. It's crucial, if he wants the relationship to last, that he fully understands her ideas and explains to her precisely how he believes his affairs fit in with them: a demanding task!

But no amount of clever talk will save the most vulnerable combination:

	Partner 1	Partner 2
Sexual personality type	Splitter	Cosmo
Second tendency	Big Boy	Donor
Third tendency	Bully	Bully

They do not see, and never have really seen, eye to eye on the dominance dimension. Initially he probably teased her flirtatiously about her forcefulness, but he doesn't really want her to fulfil her desire to be independent and self-assertive, and the teasing soon begins to annoy her. Her Bully side makes her potentially stroppy anyway, and confronted with the rejection of this independent part of her make-up, she soon begins to lose her temper when he attacks. She expects rejection where none exists; actual rejection inflames her. Yet it's necessary for the Big Boy in him to feel he controls her, and as part of *his* bullying side is to be rejecting, he's unable to stop himself even if he wanted to – which, after a short time, he doesn't because the sex no longer suits him. To start with, the sex may have been exciting – a struggle for conquest that nevertheless involved a certain acquiescence on both sides. But as the battle for power builds up and the clashes become more bitter, both revert to their natural style: he always wants to dominate, and she wants to feel more equal.

It's at this point that his splitting takes over and rapidly destroys what little affection is left. Any Little Princess Snatcher with an ounce of common sense who comes across this couple and wants to get her paws on this Splitter will walk it. Not only will he be looking eagerly (but not necessarily consciously) for the sort of person that she is, but he will also have very few scruples about it. He'll feel that the Cosmo has renounced any rights she had and may actually enjoy staying out all night and explaining precisely why. On top of all this, the Cosmo is a Donor! So she will not stand in their way and will overlook a great deal. Which doesn't mean she won't get furious sometimes and, in the end, be the one to jack it in. Off the Big Boy will go with his new partner to live unhappily ever after because as soon as he is no longer part of a triangle the sex will begin to wane again, and he's back to square one. But that's another story (see Splitter–Little Princess).

The least vulnerable combination is:

	Partner 1	Partner 2
Sexual personality type	Splitter	Cosmo
Second tendency	Wimp	Clinger
Third tendency	Clinger	Donor

The issue here is: will the Cosmo put up with her Wimp's affairs? The clinging tendency of both glues them together, and their dominance compatibility works well in and out of bed. He is less likely to have affairs, and will have fewer affairs than with any other partner, yet it's a rare Splitter who is faithful. And where there is infidelity, there are uncertainty and dissension.

Of crucial importance is how he represents his affairs to her. Unlike the Big Boy, he has no inherent need to feel more powerful, so he is less likely to use the affairs as a weapon for putting her down. Nor does he want to brag about them, so they may well go undiscovered. If he's the diplomatic, low-key sort of Wimp, there's every chance of a stable relationship. The Cosmo, of course, must be prepared to tolerate an unexciting sex life, but she may be the sort whose drive goes into other pursuits anyway – her work, being a super housewife and so forth.

At its best it can work, then, but this is rare. It is more common for the Cosmo to feel gradually less and less enchanted with the relationship and fed up with her partner's apparent lack of desire. She may try to persuade him to see a doctor or to go for joint therapy of some sort to try to get their sex life back on the road again. Unfortunately, it is his splitting that needs treatment, and unless she finds out about the affairs this won't be obvious to her.

If she does find out, there'll be heart-searching rather than screaming and shouting, and if they break up, it's most likely to be she who leaves when she discovers yet another concealed affair after he has sworn never to err again. The trust between them is liable to be irreparably damaged.

His favourite type of mistress will have Cosmo tendencies too and is often a friend of his regular partner. She will usually have pronounced Snatcher tendencies – stealing a friend's man is common in this variation. Basically he loves his regular Cosmo, and the splitting is a sad addiction that he can't seem to kick. It not only destroys their often highly valued relationship but is also a tragedy for the children.

BULLY AND DONOR

Position in league: **Eighth**
Estimated proportion of this type of couple that has
    affairs: **74%**
Most likely unfaithful: **Bully**
Most likely third party: **Clinger**

Case history

Terry, the faithful Donor
Karen, the unfaithful Bully
Paul, the third-party Wimp

In no way did Karen want it to happen. All three were good
friends. In fact, Paul still says that he wished it could have
been avoided.

Terry and Paul were close friends. They would sit up late,
talking about their lives, philosophy, wide-ranging topics.
Karen found this boring, but Terry insisted she join in. She
would do so only sometimes, making very tough, caustic and
practical contributions. She and Paul didn't really get on at
this point, but they got to know each other.

In two main ways, although there were a thousand subtle
nuances to it, Terry pushed them to it. First, he went right
off sex, and Karen was both frustrated and offended. Secondly, Terry persistently left Paul and Karen alone together
in the most tempting of situations and behaved in such an
absurd fashion that they were forced to tell him not to be
an idiot. Finally, a frustrated Karen made a spur-of-the-
moment move, and rapidly she and Paul found they were in
love. How were they to tell Terry? In the end Paul did and, to
his astonishment, was told, 'It couldn't have happened to a
nicer guy.' Terry had decided that he and Karen should have
an open relationship, and for a time this was indeed the
case – until Paul and Karen fell out of love and Karen,

fed up with the whole arrangement, moved to a new town.

Paul and Karen's love had been manufactured unwittingly by Terry and unbeknown to them. They had lived out Terry's fantasy.

Profile

The Donors who are most effective in driving their partner into another's arms are the ones who convert the Bully's rages into sexual revenge. They sneer at the Bully's sexual adequacy; they shout at the most heated moments in arguments, 'OK, if you're so bloody dissatisfied with me, go and find someone else.' ('I might just do that,' the Bully screams back); they spend a lot of time at parties drawing their partner's attention to the advantages of others who have qualities they lack just when the Bully is feeling secure and loving in the existing relationship.

Crucial is the strength of the Bully's splitting tendency. If it's the third tendency, the Donor's actions will be experienced as rejection but are less likely to prompt infidelity. In these circumstances compatibility on the other dimensions will be the key. A Bully second tendency in the Donor makes things worse, and a Big Boy–Cosmo dominance incompatibility is fatal. But at the heart of the relationship will be a constant niggle for the Bully – the Donor's behaviour feels like rejection.

The most vulnerable combination is as follows:

	Partner 1	Partner 2
Sexual personality type	Bully	Donor
Second tendency	Splitter	Bully
Third tendency	Big Boy	Cosmo

She keeps telling him she wants to lead an independent life. She does nothing to prevent him from chatting up Little Princesses at parties, adopting a haughty 'He's like a little boy' attitude to it. She tends to run herself down, and her timing is poor when it comes to key events.

The sex is quite refreshing at first, yet it rapidly turns into a battle. Worst of all, she goes out of her way to introduce him to a corking Little Princess friend.

It ends badly. She bawls him out repeatedly, not about the affairs – which she accepts with surprising equanimity, in her friends' view – but about other seemingly insignificant matters: lateness, lack of tidiness, not pulling his weight about the house. He gives her as good as he gets, and for the first few months she backs down; the day (or night) she doesn't is the one on which he packs his bags or storms off to seek consolation in the arms of his favourite Princess.

The least vulnerable combination:

	Partner 1	Partner 2
Sexual personality type	Bully	Donor
Second tendency	Big Boy	Clinger
Third tendency	Splitter	Little Princess

He expects rejection, she to be abandoned. His masterful, 'I wear the trousers' side laps up her clinging, which compensates for life's blows to his esteem. She makes him feel good, and he makes her feel safe.

The key is how much, and in what ways, she tries to donate him to womankind. If her Donor tendency is very strong, she may create situations that are just too tempting. If her behaviour makes him angry rather than sexy, then it may well be ineffectual – they have rows because he feels rejected, but he does not use sex as part of the rows. He simply complains about her to anyone who will listen.

The outcome of this version of the Bully–Donor couple depends a lot on luck: if a more compatible, wily Snatcher happens on the Bully at the right time, in the right place, an accident may happen, especially if the Donor is there and runs herself down in a way that both irritates the Bully and enhances the attractiveness of the Snatcher. But with luck and good timing it can work out well, and the Donor's self-destructive potential will remain unrealized.

Overall, the most likely third parties (particularly if the Donor has a Bully second tendency) are Clingers skilled at snatching and more compatible on the dominance dimension. To snatch effectively, the Donor's gifts of power and status must be used to the full by the third party, and the Bully's feelings of rejection put to good use too. He'll moan about his partner; the Snatcher's trick is subtly to convert consolation into desire.

SPLITTER AND LITTLE PRINCESS

Position in league: **Ninth**
Estimated proportion of this type of couple that has
   affairs: **72%**
Most likely unfaithful: **Splitter**
Most likely third party: **Someone who is compatible on
   dominance dimension**

Case history

Sophie, the faithful Little Princess
Barry, the unfaithful Splitter
Jackie, the third-party Cosmo

Barry was an easy-going, slightly childlike lad who drifted into marriage to Sophie when both were only twenty. But for all his Wimpish diffidence, there was one thing Barry did care about strongly: sex.

Sophie: 'Barry always was very keen on sex but not in a pushy way. The only trouble was that he did tend to want me to do all the work. At first I didn't mind, but after a bit I did rather wish he'd be a bit more dominant.'

Barry: 'I have a lot of fantasies – I always have. Sophie was part of what I call my "luscious" fantasy. She's slightly plump, a very homely sort of woman. My dream was always for that very feminine kind of woman to seduce me. But that sort of woman doesn't want to do that.

'Now, Jackie is quite different. She isn't really "luscious". She is tall and thin and has been totally in control of me from day one. I was hooked from the moment she took charge.'

Jackie: 'Barry isn't right for Sophie. She's still living in the Middle Ages – a maiden waiting for her knight. Well, I'm more of a knight than either of them because I know what I want. And I wanted Barry.

'I met him at a party. He seemed shy and quiet. He was just looking about him as if he wasn't all there. I could tell he wasn't really as vague as that because there was a knowing look in his eye. I studied him while talking to someone else. Then when the chance came and I was introduced, I told him to get me another drink. He was startled but got it. I pretended to be a bit submissive and, sure enough, he asked me where I worked. He knows I can please him in a way that Sophie never will.

'I've told him that he can't leave Sophie yet. Only when he's more able to think for himself will I let him. But I think we've got a future together – maybe.'

But Barry has the last word: 'The reality of a truly dominant woman isn't the same as my fantasies. I know what it's really like now, and I think that's enough. I don't tell Sophie much, but it's obvious she knows and that she hurts. I do love her and I don't want this affair with Jackie to go on much longer.'

Profile

At one extreme this is a natural and, at times, contented coupling that works; at the other it's hell on earth during the short time it lasts.

Little Princessess often believe that men are like animals. They do not find male infidelity puzzling or surprising, but that doesn't mean they necessarily like or accept it when they're cheated on.

The Little Princess's reaction depends on her second and third tendencies. If she has a Bully second tendency, she's far more likely to sniff out peccadilloes and vehemently protest at them, whereas a Clinger second tendency will make her less likely to look for trouble; given the fear of abandonment, the Clinger feels that she doesn't want to risk losing him by even thinking that he might be having affairs. A Donor second tendency makes her more likely to adopt a 'boys will be boys' attitude.

If she's living with a Wimp, whatever her second tendency she's going to be uncomfortable with him, and they will grow apart; his splitting will speed up this process. If he's got pronounced Bully tendencies, she's not going to like that either – *ugly* scenes are not her style – and she will be more prepared to give him the boot when she gets wind of affairs.

So at one extreme the most vulnerable coupling is:

	Partner 1	Partner 2
Sexual personality type	Splitter	Little Princess
Second tendency	Wimp	Donor
Third tendency	Bully	Bully

What was his original attraction for her? Something superficial must have blinded her to his incompatibility. Almost certainly she had no idea about his Bully side, but intuitively her Donor desires sniffed out a potential Splitter, and *this actually attracted her*. But so did something else: perhaps exceptional good looks; power, status, wealth or all three (maybe they work together and he seems impressive); perhaps he was her best friend's ex-boyfriend and the affair was to do with displaced desires.

Whatever the original cause, the effect is a desultory relationship. Principally there's a rumbling tone of bitterness just beneath the surface (the Bully–Bully third tendencies) and a sense of mismatch which makes her Donor behaviour more effective. At a party she introduces him to a Cosmo friend who, if she fancies a snatch, will be on to a winner; he will find the Cosmo an exciting contrast.

In the end the relationship just peters out. Either he goes off with a Cosmo, or they just pack it in by mutual consent, but whichever it is a bad taste is left in the mouth, and in unguarded moments each can be pretty sarcastic about the other even years later.

The least vulnerable version is:

	Partner 1	Partner 2
Sexual personality type	Splitter	Little Princess
Second tendency	Big Boy	Clinger
Third tendency	Clinger	Donor

If this one comes unstuck, both will be very saddened. The key is her attitude to his affairs. Does she turn a blind eye and put it down to hormones? Or is there a permanent state of lip-biting tension as she sits waiting for him – she has a Clinger second tendency – long after she knows he's left the office?

It all depends on how he goes about the affairs. He mustn't rub her face in them if he wants to keep it going. Which by and large he does. He may long to be rid of his wanderlust and even seek treatment for it – he may feel he hasn't grown up properly.

These two love each other, and his affairs are a tragedy if they break up the whole family, children and all. As Clinger types they *want* it to work, and she's prepared to ignore a lot to keep it going.

The Snatcher is a very sinister figure in this scenario. Often he's the happily married man, she the younger woman (the secretary of fable). She senses his lust for her quickly. She realizes the vulnerability of the partner. She knows she can reel him in, and, in a good proportion of tragic cases, because the opportunity is there she takes it. Envy, greed and other ugly motives cause her to steal and destroy something good. It can be a tragedy all ways round because, once she's snatched him, her interest dwindles rapidly in most cases.

SPLITTER AND BIG BOY

Position in league: **Tenth**
Estimated proportion of this type of couple that has
    affairs: **72%**
Most likely unfaithful: **Splitter**
Most likely third party: **Little Princess Snatcher**

Case history

Danny, the faithful Big Boy
Karen, the unfaithful Splitter
George, the third-party Clinger

As a Splitter, Karen liked seducing men. She wasn't so
much promiscuous as aggressively flirtatious. That's
what attracted Danny in the first place, but not long after
their second child's birth it led to some terrible rows
between them. It was in the aftermath of just such a row
that Karen had her first affair. This got her started on a
career of marital infidelity which Danny can do nothing to
prevent.

Danny: 'Only old age will stop Karen from being unfaithful. I've got a stark choice: get out or lump it. I've decided to
do the latter because I can't face the damage I'd do to the
children, but it's less than ideal.

'The strange thing is, the sure-fire way to tell if Karen's got
an affair on the boil is when she's keen on sex with me. Like
now, for example, she's involved with some bloke called
George. I know his name because he keeps leaving messages
for her to ring him – some nerve! Well, up until recently, she
was right off sex. Now she's dead keen.' (Danny's Donor
tendency has helped him accept the situation.)

Karen: 'I used to look on it as a problem with a capital P, as
though I was a nympho or something. I mean, I've always
enjoyed the joys of flirting, but now I've really accepted how I

am. What's wrong with it? I love Danny, but I'd only make him unhappy if I was unhappy too.

'Take the present situation. George is really good-looking. He's a bit younger than I am, and he's supple and strong. He doesn't want to marry me but I suppose we're becoming very fond of each other in a limited way. I keep it from Danny when we meet, and there's all the thrill of doing something that shouldn't really be done.

'You'd think I'd feel odd when I go back to Danny, but it isn't like that. Danny's Danny; George is George. In fact, I can enjoy Danny more because he feels fresher if I've been with George. I like things the way they are.'

Profile

Your Big Boy's pride is easily injured, and a partner's affairs are the most injurious. He does not think of himself as the type to be cuckolded. If anybody does the playing around, he feels, it should be him. Only with the greatest tact will she get away with it, and only if there is a lot else to keep them together will it last. It all depends on the match between their respective second and third tendencies.

Looked at from the outside, the partners seem very separate; there doesn't appear to be much communication between them. He goes gaily about his Big Boy business, like sports and hobbies or extremely hard work late and at weekends; she keeps mum about her affairs and lots of other things besides – the dent in the car, the new pair of shoes they can't afford and so on.

At its most vulnerable, in this couple he quickly feels dissatisfied:

	Partner 1	Partner 2
Sexual personality type	Splitter	Big Boy
Second tendency	Cosmo	Donor
Third tendency	Bully	Bully

In principle, each is not generally attracted to the sort of person the other is. Some combination of things like wealth, status and good looks got them together, and it's only later on that they realize the mistake they've made. As a Donor, he subconsciously senses her Splitter tendency and is perhaps attracted by it: at one level he feels it's right that she has affairs; at another, the Big Boy part of him hates it and feels humiliated.

But, worst of all, their incompatibility on the dominance dimension and their Bully–Bully pairing create an ever-growing bitterness that ends in tears. In bed it may be exciting at first, but excitement rapidly disintegrates into a struggle for dominance. They feel very frustrated after the early tolerance that marks all sex at the start has passed. Gradually she is liable to see him as more and more of a male chauvinist and he to feel she's a savage harridan who wants to castrate him. They clash over values and begin to make bitchy comments in public or to argue openly and furiously.

Her affairs are the last straw. As the situation deteriorates, she uses them more and more to attack him. The worst thing is that his Donor side actually promotes them. It's torture for the Big Boy in him to see another man possess her and yet part of him feels it's right. In the end he will probably walk out after a blazing argument, possibly about her affairs, equally possibly about politics or a longstanding bone of contention like who drinks and who drives on a night out. The row is only a symptom of their deep incompatibility.

The least vulnerable version of this couple never works very well either:

	Partner 1	Partner 2
Sexual personality type	Splitter	Big Boy
Second tendency	Little Princess	Donor
Third tendency	Clinger	Bully

His forcefulness fits her well. He is probably a bit of a bull in a china shop, oblivious to a lot of what goes on around him. So long as she's tactful and clever, she can keep the relationship going for as long as she wants. He doesn't fully appreciate the extent of her duplicity and, when glimpsing it, can usually be fobbed off with false explanations. She gets a big kick out of their kissing and making up, excited by the idea of deceiving him so well. The relationship is a cycle of deception – discovery – repossession (he thinks). That he never has her all to himself makes it all the more of a thrill.

They will come unstuck if she's not bright enough or naturally tactless. When she runs out of tricks and he loses faith in her oft-broken promises, he will get extremely annoyed and storm out or she will head off for good with one of her lovers. He may indulge in recriminations for years afterwards; she will forget him more easily.

The Third Party is unlikely to be anything other than a Big Boy Snatcher. She has a great time with him until she leaves her original partner. Then, for her, the whole cycle repeats itself.

DONOR AND COSMO

Position in league: **Eleventh**
Estimated proportion of this type of couple that has
 affairs: **68%**
Most likely unfaithful: **Cosmo**
Most likely third party: **Wimp Snatcher**

Case history

Charlie, the faithful Donor
Tina, the unfaithful Cosmo
Dave, the third-party Wimp

For eight years Charlie's and Tina's marriage seemed solid and satisfying. Sadly, there was a time-bomb ticking away that was to damage irreparably their trust and love for each other. The canker of Charlie's Donor tendencies took eight years to strike.

Tina: 'When our oldest was aged four, Charlie started going on and on about how I should get back to work, get out more and see more people. I was perfectly happy, in fact, and the only argument I could see for it was that we needed the money. Eventually I gave in and he got me a part-time job in the college where he works and where I used to work as a research assistant. To begin with, it was hard, but soon I was glad that he'd encouraged me to do it. We used to have lunch together a lot with one of Charlie's colleagues, Dave. Now, Dave and I worked on the same subject – which was why Charlie had introduced us – and we soon got into heated debates about various topics. It was Charlie, I think, who first suggested that we do something about these disputes. "Why not apply for a grant?" he said. "Why not test out which of you is right?" Well, that's what we did.

'The study was of reproduction in frogs, and our dispute was whether frogs deliberately choose particular mates or whether it's a random matter. Of course, the ironies of this subject weren't obvious to me then.

'Dave would always be asking me to work late or to go out for a drink after we'd finished. I would tell him I had to get back to Charlie and the kids. But when I told Charlie that Dave was being a bit of a pest, his reaction surprised me: "Look, it's important for your work that you keep him happy, so I'll stay in and look after the kids, and you look after the boss."

'Of course, I liked Dave – everyone does. He had lovely hair and nice hands. But I'd never seriously considered a romance with anyone apart from Charlie. Well, I suppose Charlie was being a bit dull, and I felt a bit insulted when he actually encouraged me to pander to Dave, as if he didn't care for me. So I thought, "All right, I *will* go out for a few drinks with Dave." It was only a matter of time before things went further.'

Charlie: 'She planned it from the start. I see the whole thing now. She got that research grant to work with Dave so they could have an affair. And all that stuff about needing to work late! How obvious can you get? She has the cheek to say I encouraged her when it's as plain as anything – she deliberately set out to have an affair with my friend Dave. It's as simple as that.'

Dave: 'I feel bad about Charlie, and I know I've hurt him. It's very cruel the way things sometimes work out. But it isn't anyone's fault. It just happened. No one schemed or plotted. It's as if it was meant to be.'

Profile

This couple can work out well where the Cosmo's infidelity is seen by both partners as a natural extension of her inclination to be independent. 'I live my life; she lives hers,' the Donor will say with a philosophical shrug of his shoulders. 'So long as she doesn't threaten our relationship, it really doesn't bother me if she has affairs. I wouldn't want to restrict her because I love her.' From a Wimp this comes more easily than from a Big Boy, but a Donor of either type is prone to this sort of attitude. It actually suits his desire to donate her.

That doesn't mean it's easy for either of them. It's a tightrope. She may fall into the arms of another man; he may fall into a mixed state of depression and rage if he's not careful, torn between feeling exploited and a desire for her to be unfaithful. There's no safety net for this couple.

There is also another danger. She loves him very much indeed and has no desire whatsoever to be unfaithful. If she has a Bully second tendency, his attempts to donate her to other men will seem like rejection and will make her unstable and difficult. And whether a Bully or not, no one likes being subtly encouraged to sleep with other partners if he or she is happy with an existing one.

The most vulnerable couple always ends in confusion and anger:

	Partner 1	Partner 2
Sexual personality type	Donor	Cosmo
Second tendency	Big Boy	Splitter
Third tendency	Bully	Bully

Initially, they pay little attention to each other's personalities. Other factors are more important. Maybe one of them is rich, powerful or of high status and the other exceptionally attractive. Whatever the initial buzz, it wears off rapidly as the clashes on the dominance dimension – their different values and their assertive style – become irreconcilable. That both have Bully tendencies makes these clashes even worse. Soon the relationship is one long battle for supremacy. There is nothing satisfying for either, and she embarks on a series of affairs.

As the relationship slides inexorably towards termination, they row increasingly. They come to hate each other the more they get to know about their bullying and incompatible sides. It ends in tears.

At its least vulnerable, it looks like this:

	Partner 1	Partner 2
Sexual personality type	Donor	Cosmo
Second tendency	Wimp	Clinger
Third tendency	Clinger	Splitter

This Wimp can feel quite content so long as the Cosmo *does* have affairs. If she doesn't, both get very frustrated. He becomes neurotic, and she eventually realizes that he's not for her. If she does, he needs to be the sort of person who doesn't mind sharing her with others. If so, he's quite a passive man who is happy to put her first in all things. His friends have sometimes wondered whether he's gay – he may be a slight and rather invisible type of man. The Cosmo, a forceful, possibly charming woman, may also be bisexual in spirit if not in practice.

The attractions of a Wimp third party without Donor tendencies will be considerable to a Cosmo in this couple whatever the combination of the other tendencies. She's less vulnerable to a Snatcher if she and the Donor are both Clingers – clinging unites them literally and metaphorically.

DONOR AND BIG BOY

Position in league: **Twelfth**
Estimated proportion of this type of couple that has
   affairs: **68%**
Most likely unfaithful: **Big Boy**
Most likely third party: **Little Princess Snatcher**

Case history

Vanessa, the faithful Donor
Jim, the unfaithful Big Boy
Sharon, the third-party Little Princess

Vanessa never felt as beguilingly sexy as her sister Sharon. To
outsiders Vanessa seemed very sweet with her brown bob of
hair and petite figure. That Sharon was tall, leggy and blonde
didn't actually make her more desirable than her sister – lots
of their men friends went for Vanessa rather than Sharon. Yet
that wasn't how Vanessa saw it. She had the kind of inferi-
ority complex that we have often seen in daughters of youthful, Joan Collins-type mothers. And, indeed, Vanessa's
mother was the true cause of the problem: she made her
daughter feel insignificant and had always done so. Sadly,
this led to Vanessa's donating her greatest love to someone
she imagined was her superior – her sister Sharon.

  Jim: 'Vanessa and I had been going steady for about three
years when we went on holiday to Greece. Sharon was between boyfriends, and without even consulting me Vanessa
took pity on her and invited her to come too. I had been
looking forward to some time alone with Vanessa, so I was
rather irritated.

  'I've never been keen on tourism – ruins and paintings and
all that – so when we got to the island all I wanted to do was
stretch out on the beach. Vanessa would set off early every
morning to do her sightseeing, and to start with Sharon went

with her. That suited me fine. But then Sharon began to get fed up with all those bits of stone and guide books and Vanessa said she didn't mind at all if her sister preferred to laze on the beach.

'There I was, stuck on this beach with Sharon every day. Until then I'd never much gone for her. I felt she was a bit stuck up and stand-offish, but soon I was rubbing the oil on her back for her, just for a bit of a laugh, something to do between chapters as I ploughed my way through another Jeffrey Archer. Suddenly it wasn't a game any more. I think I was feeling very frustrated by Vanessa, and maybe angry with her, and Sharon *is* a very sexy girl.'

Sharon: 'Afterwards I felt awful. I mean he was my *sister*'s boyfriend. But Vanessa didn't seem to notice anything. She didn't make us feel guilty, and I thought, "Was it my fault that we were left alone like that all the time? Was it my fault they weren't really getting on with each other?" OK, it split them up, but wouldn't it have happened anyway?'

Profile

Your Big Boy tends to think of himself as a natural Jack the Lad. Although in practice he may be loving and faithful and very reluctant to stray, he may go in for rowdy sexual badinage with his mates. Thus if his partner does encourage him to be unfaithful, it squares with his idea of himself as a bit of a Don Juan.

However, if he has Bully tendencies, he may feel very rejected by her behaviour. What she more or less deliberately intends as an attempt to persuade him that he could be doing better than her in his choice of partners he experiences as a critical comment on him. This leads, almost inevitably, to rows.

The key to this couple, therefore, is the degree to which the Big Boy wants to have affairs and the way in which the different tendencies of both partners combine. Underlying the whole situation is the Donor's tendency to run herself down and set up other women as more desirable than she is.

For some arrogant and lustful Big Boys this is a perfect arrangement: it suits their vanity and desire to cheat (though they hardly need to cheat, so easy does the Donor make it). For others it's a sad situation. They can't understand why their partner keeps rejecting them.

At its most vulnerable the couple looks like this:

	Partner 1	*Partner 2*
Sexual personality type	Donor	Big Boy
Second tendency	Cosmo	Splitter
Third tendency	Bully	Bully

Their incompatibility is complete. Other factors bind them together initially, such as money or power or good looks.

When clashes on the dominance dimension become the most prominent aspect of the relationship, nothing can save it. The Donor/Cosmo justifies his affairs by telling herself that it is an independent, adult relationship. Unfortunately, only he is sexually independent in reality, but she carefully ignores this fact.

Their Bully tendencies make the power struggle worse. He consoles himself with a series of affairs; she feels both embarrassed and secretly satisfied.

As the relationship grows increasingly hostile, the quarrels become more bitter and more frequent. The Bully in each hates the Bully in the other.

At its least vulnerable the couple looks like this:

	Partner 1	*Partner 2*
Sexual personality type	Donor	Big Boy
Second tendency	Little Princess	Clinger
Third tendency	Clinger	Splitter

This Donor/Little Princess may feel quite content with her Big Boy's affairs. She understands his needs and doesn't mind sharing him with others. She's quite a passive woman, who is pleased to ensure his happiness.

The attractions of a Little Princess third party without the Donor tendencies will be considerable to a Big Boy in this couple, whatever the combination of the other tendencies. He's less vulnerable to a Snatcher if he and the Donor are both Clingers.

BIG BOY AND COSMO

Position in league: **Thirteenth**
Estimated proportion of this type of couple that has affairs: **67%**
Most likely unfaithful: **Big Boy in least vulnerable combinations**
Cosmo in most vulnerable combinations
Most likely third party: **Wimp or Little Princess**

Case history

Teddy, the faithful Big Boy
Geraldine, the unfaithful Cosmo
Crispin, the third-party Wimp

In her mid-fifties something extraordinary happened to Geraldine: she became independent and successful. Her country solicitor husband Teddy never really accepted the new wife she became and, with deep regret, she left him.

Geraldine: 'About five years ago my life revolved around exam results. The youngest was coming up to O-levels, and the oldest was taking his degree. All I ever seemed to think about was small slips of paper that might ambush one of my beloved children and send them into the depths of depression or transports of joy.

'Realizing that the day when there would be no more results because there were no more children was not far away, I decided in a small way to do something myself: I joined my local Tory party. Ted was delighted, and I began a life of fund-raising balls and party events. I was surprised to discover that I liked that life and was quite good at it. In a short time I rose in the hierarchy, and soon I was chairing meetings and contributing to local policy documents. Teddy began to complain a bit when I wasn't home for dinner on three consecutive nights but that wasn't really what was annoying him. Looking back, I can see it was the fact that we'd never really been suited, that while I was the "little wife" things were fine, but now that I was an active, high-profile member of the community, with my pictures in the local paper and so forth, I was a threat.

'The local election campaign that led to my becoming a councillor caused some very stiff rows between us. For days on end we didn't speak. At dinner parties he began making carping comments about "Mrs T. and her monstrous regiment of wives". I was not amused. It was so childish, so like Teddy – too immature to share his life with a real adult. I think that when Crispin came along it was really all over between Teddy and me, though neither of us would have admitted it at the time.'

Teddy: 'She will, of course, give you a very different story, very different indeed. But if you want to know the truth, I'll tell it to you. She is not the woman I married, and the reason is simple: the mid-life crisis. She simply could not cope with the changes in her body, with the fact that once she was young and beautiful and now she is, well, no spring chicken.

'I bear her and Crispin no malice. Good luck to Crispin – he'll need it! In my view, her head's so full of madcap ideas – *political* ideas, I ask you – that I should think she needs treatment. But that's not my problem.

'I'm a hard-working professional and have been for many years. She'll tell you I'm against women working. Well, I'm not; in fact, we appointed a lady partner in our firm only last year. But she didn't have any other responsibilities. Geraldine did and does. When we married we agreed that was how it should be: I would earn the money – and God knows I've forked out a lot of it for her and the children, not that I begrudge it – and she would look after the home. She's simply not stuck to her side of the bargain. She has a duty to me and the children. How would *she* have felt if *I*'d given up work and stopped bringing in the money?'

Profile

This is likely to be a fight to the finish. The partners' similar styles of aggression and different values and sexual identities produce a battle royal. It may be fought out over all three dissonant aspects, or it may be most prominent in one special area. If the clash is most virulent over sex – he wants her to be more passive and she wants to be more active – that makes infidelity an even bigger risk: she really wants a Wimp and he a Little Princess, but neither may realize it for a long time, if ever. The Cosmo's love of independence runs smack into the Big Boy's wish to possess her. It makes her marginally more likely overall to seek a lover in order to prove her freedom.

On the other hand, if they settle into a domesticated life, perhaps with children, then the Big Boy becomes a more likely bet for infidelity – he may feel it's his right. But on the whole he's a great one for homemaking, and he knows that a self-willed, independent Cosmo won't put up with any nonsense.

In the least vulnerable combination the two of them are bound together, despite their incompatibility, by clinging:

	Partner 1	Partner 2
Sexual personality type	Big Boy	Cosmo
Second tendency	Clinger	Clinger
Third tendency	Donor	Splitter

If married, this couple may be faithful because each needs the other to cling on to. Perhaps he works hard and she has her hands full with children and, as soon as she can, a job again. Yes, there is running, rumbling discord on certain issues – like whether to move to a different area or whether he pulls his weight about the house – and sometimes they have blazing rows, but in the end neither dares seek a new partner because they both *need* each other out of insecurity. In addition, it's important that he's the Donor in this combination: he probably gets more chance to be unfaithful than she – *he* doesn't have to get back to pick up the kids from school. So this combination can get along without any infidelity, and permutations of it make up most of the 30 per cent or so of Big Boy–Cosmo couples who stay faithful.

At the other extreme is this combination:

	Partner 1	Partner 2
Sexual personality type	Big Boy	Cosmo
Second tendency	Bully	Splitter
Third tendency	Donor	Bully

The combination of bullying tendencies in both partners and his Big Boy values and sexual identity makes this a recipe for Cosmo infidelity, especially since she's a Splitter and even more if she's under 30. She bitterly resents the way he pushes her around. He acts as if she doesn't know how to run her own life. If she wasn't a feminist before the relationship started, the chances are that she's moved a good deal in that direction since it did. She has a Bully third tendency, and this adds fuel to the fire – sometimes she gets absolutely livid, as opposed to just angry, as a result. It's not long before she is longing to be freer but, on top of that, she's going to put him in his place. The chances are that she teaches him a lesson by flinging a Wimp in his face ('At least Bill doesn't treat me like some kind of Victorian chattel. I don't belong to you, you know,' she will tell her Big Boy).

Between these two extremes lie various uncomfortable compromises, but in the end only a minority of this type of couple are able to overcome their incompatibility on the dominance dimension. A Wimp beckons the Cosmo, and for the Big Boy a Little Princess will be a great relief. A Snatcher can take advantage of the situation, but only if he or she has submissive or Clinger tendencies. Neither the Big Boy nor the Cosmo is looking to make matters worse with a Bully Snatcher or to repeat the mistake with another Cosmo or Big Boy.

DONOR AND WIMP

Position in league: **Fourteenth**
Estimated proportion of this type of couple that has
   affairs: **66%**
Most likely unfaithful: **Wimp**
Most likely third party: **Cosmo Snatcher**

General profile

Julie, the faithful Donor
Roger, the unfaithful Wimp
Helen, the third-party Cosmo Snatcher

When Roger met Julie Roger's and Helen's marriage had been over for five years. They saw each other rarely, and then usually in a work context and perhaps for a drink afterwards. There had long since ceased to be either desire or hostility between them. If ever they did discuss what went wrong between them, it was always to agree that they had never been right for each other; they were too similar in their ambitions, and it was a mercy that they had had no children.

Julie was very different from Helen. When she first arrived at Roger's office to work as his secretary he paid her scant notice. She was unprepossessing in appearance and unobtrusive in manner. His life at that time revolved solely around his work; his domestic comforts were few and his private life non-existent. For although he felt no bitterness concerning his first marriage, he also felt reluctant to commit himself again.

Roger first began to notice Julie through various small

considerations she showed in the arrangements she organized for him. She had obviously studied his tastes and habits and used her observations to make the running of his life subtly smoother. He was touched by this and began to take more notice of her. So that one evening, after they had been working late at the office, he noticed she looked tired and somewhat despondent and in a spontaneous gesture asked her if she'd care to dine with him.

Their courtship was slow but sure: Julie's diffidence and low self-esteem had constantly to be eroded by Roger's certainty that they could be happy together. Two years after Julie came to work for Roger they were married in a quiet, unostentatious ceremony.

Roger's second marriage could not have been more different from his first. Julie gave up work to make him a wonderful home that he was always grateful to return to and, in the fullness of time, bore him two sons whom they both adored. And yet she could never quite break free from the conviction that she was not good enough for him. Try as he might to convince her of the contrary, Julie clung to the belief that Roger's tempestuous, jet-setting life with Helen had been more to his taste.

So it was with a certain grim satisfaction that Julie greeted the news that Helen's firm was to be doing business with Roger's and that their meetings would be frequent. Now he would discover which wife he preferred! And far better to face the danger than to be constantly living in fear of it, she felt. Not privy to Julie's fantasies, Roger was perplexed by her evident wish to throw him and Helen together at every possible opportunity.

But, sure enough, as time passed Julie's tearful passivity began to show to marked disadvantage by comparison with Helen's breezy self-confidence. Roger is now distraught to find himself, after seven years of contented married life, hankering after an alternative that he knows does not really suit him. It is a ghastly predicament; he knows neither how he got into it nor how to get out of it.

Profile

The key to this couple's success is the nature of the Wimp. The Donor puts herself down. She may go to extreme lengths to prove to herself and him that he would be better with someone else or at least having an affair. She may dress badly, get fat, have ugly habits – all to express her feelings of unworthiness and inadequacy. She may foster affairs between him and other women.

Some Wimps are loving and don't want to have affairs. Some are passive and diffident and will just ignore the Donor's behaviour. Others are quite sly sexual adventurers. Others still place great emphasis on being independent and see it as a matter of principle that they and their partners can have an affair if they want to, so long as it doesn't destroy the relationship. But mostly Wimps do not like being encouraged to have affairs. They like to have meaningful relationships.

The sort of Wimp he is dictates how he reacts to her encouragement to have affairs.

At its most vulnerable the couple looks like this:

	Partner 1	Partner 2
Sexual personality type	Donor	Wimp
Second tendency	Little Princess	Splitter
Third tendency	Bully	Bully

This sort of Wimp is not averse to sliding into bed with a friend after an evening out together. It's not very hard for the Donor to ease this along – leaving early with a headache when it's obvious he fancies someone else, not asking him where he got to last night and so on.

They don't get along too well anyway. In bed they are both very tentative. Neither takes the lead. Initial pleasure in the lack of pressure probably soon drifts into apathy and passivity. He's not getting on with her out of bed either. Neither likes open rows, but there's a lot of tension under the surface. It may be only little things that seem to irk them: maybe she insists on cooking for him *every* night, when he'd like to do it sometimes and, at others, would prefer to snack it. They don't violently disagree about ideas except when their Bully sides come out. If she's persistently late, there will come a time when he loses his temper but storms off rather than shouting at her. Or they may play the game of being late for each other and be quite unable to talk it out. In the end they may find it hard to meet at all, literally or emotionally. It's at this point that the third-party Snatcher, who presents a strong contrast to the Donor, will succeed if she suggests he move in with her.

At its least vulnerable this couple arrives at a cosy but passionless stalemate:

	Partner 1	Partner 2
Sexual personality type	Donor	Wimp
Second tendency	Cosmo	Clinger
Third tendency	Clinger	Splitter

They cling together and enjoy each other's company, yet she will keep trying to prise them apart. He cannot understand why she keeps putting him in compromising positions with women who make passes at him, and he finds it even more incomprehensible that she laughs it off when he tells her about it.

For her part, she may be troubled by fantasies of him with other women; she may even enjoy imagining this scenario. Being 'honest', they talk about their problems and why she doesn't feel fully settled. It may be that when they have children the problem disappears into the background and only re-emerges as an issue fifteen years later.

A strong, wily Snatcher with Cosmo tendencies may be able to take advantage of the situation, but she has to pick her moment with care. Ideally, it's just after he's been abandoned by his existing partner and needs someone to cling to. His Clinger feelings of abandonment make him depressed and in need of reassurance. If the Snatcher gets it right, she'll convert friendship into an affair.

CLINGER AND LITTLE PRINCESS

Position in league: **Fifteenth**
Estimated proportion of this type of couple that has
   affairs: **65%**
Most likely unfaithful: **Little Princess**
Most likely third party: **Big Boy**

Case history

Stephen, the faithful Clinger
Suzi, the unfaithful Little Princess
Ralph, the third-party Big Boy

Suzi was 25 when she started training as a nurse. She had
already played the field, but now being several years older
than most of the other girls on her course suddenly made her
feel old and ready to settle down. Stephen was unlike any of
the boys she had been with before. He had been educated at
one of the top public schools and had then gone straight to
medical school at 18. Although he had never really lived at
home (he went to boarding school when he was 7), he had
never really left home either, and while he was more intelli-
gent, socially at ease and worldly wise than she, he was far
younger than even his twenty-three years. It was these
paradoxes, along with his aristocratic good looks, that first
fascinated and attracted her. When he showed signs of
becoming serious about her, Suzi could not believe her luck
and felt sure this was the true love she had been waiting for.

   The fact that Stephen's parents evidently disapproved of
Suzi was unfortunate but in some ways made the affair more
romantic, and the loyalty Stephen showed during their engagement made Suzi love him all the more. Secretly she
believed that Stephen's domineering mother was jealous of
Stephen's love for her and could not help preening herself a
little, and even flirting slightly with Stephen's father, just to

rub the point in. The period of their engagement was one of the happiest times of Suzi's life: she felt she had the world at her feet, with her handsome, adoring fiancé and the prospect of an enviably glamorous life ahead of them. So where did they go wrong?

Suzi: 'I loved Stephen, I really did. I mean, I still do. And I never wanted to hurt him. But he really drove me to it. In the first place, because of all those hours he worked, sleeping at the hospital, being called in in the middle of the night on his bleeper, I barely saw him. And our sex life when he was around didn't make up for his absences. And then there was his jealousy. He was like a little kid. In a way I was flattered, but those friends of his that he suspected me of flirting with – it was almost more of an insult. Which was why my head really turned when I saw Ralph. Among all those chinless wonders he looked like Clint Eastwood. And he was as rich as all of them, but he'd made it himself, which I respected more. But what a lady killer! I didn't have to explain the situation to him – he was an old hand. Oh why did Stephen ever have to find out? It would only have been a roll in the hay (neither of us wanted more), but Stephen could never understand that. For him it was the end. And now I've lost everything: my comfortable, secure life with Stephen, my fling with Ralph. But what really grates is the fact that Stephen's mother now thinks that she was right about me all along, that I'm just a cheap tart out for the main chance.'

Profile

Your Little Princess does not expect her man to be an abject, jumpy wreck every time he fears he might lose her, especially when she has no intention of abandoning him. At first she may find his little-boyish vulnerability sweet or charming, but before long she loses respect for him, feels he ought to get a grip and act like a grown-up. *She* wants to be the one who receives strong, silent support – she doesn't want to be doling it out and particularly when there seems no reason for it.

However, his clinging is merely one aspect of their relationship. At one extreme it can be the only irritant in an otherwise quite satisfactory couple. If he can control himself by understanding why he is so fearful, he can stop it from spoiling everything. At the other extreme it can be a running sore in a badly wounded relationship that will soon become a corpse. The more he clings, the more she wants to be free and the more insecure he feels and so on.

At its most vulnerable the couple looks like this:

	Partner 1	Partner 2
Sexual personality type	Clinger	Little Princess
Second tendency	Donor	Splitter
Third tendency	Wimp	Bully

This Little Princess is annoyed by the clinging and feels suffocated. She uses sex with other men as her escape because she has a Splitter second tendency. Incompatibility in values and sexual style fuels the fire of her discontent. She does not feel comfortable with his Wimpishness, combined with his pitiful insecurity, and she quickly begins to find Big Boys desirable. Sex with the Wimp was never very exciting. He always wants to cuddle her and be cuddled. While that was once quite refreshing, she's sick of it now. Big Boys' open flirtation and forcefulness seem even more sexy than before.

For the Wimp it's a vicious circle. He knows that if he wants to hang on to her, he's got to stop the clinging, yet he can't get away from the feeling that she's going to dump him. It's terrifying to him to know that what he is doing is pushing her away, yet he is unable to stop himself. He can feel her recoiling; he can feel himself reaching out; he holds ever tighter; she resists even more; and a disastrous tension develops. He is very saddened when she finally leaves with a Big Boy and will probably become very depressed. He may follow her about or ring her up at all hours of the day and night.

At its least vulnerable the couple looks like this:

	Partner 1	*Partner 2*
Sexual personality type	Clinger	Little Princess
Second tendency	Big Boy	Clinger
Third tendency	Splitter	Donor

Although the clinging is an irritant here, there are enough good things to offset it. Because the Clinger has splitting tendencies, the Little Princess is far less likely to use sex as her means to escape at the times when his clinging makes her feel trapped. For his part, he's very unlikely to embark on affairs because Clingers are terrified of losing their partner as a result.

In bed she enjoys her Clinger/Big Boy and puts up with the cuddling, although she wishes he wouldn't be so soppy at such times. They settle into a comfortable pattern, broken only by his outbreaks of insecurity.

A skilled Snatcher will be able to break up this couple. He is unlikely to be a Wimp, but the right kind of Big Boy can crack it. He needs to realize that his strength lies in the contrast he offers to the existing partner's Clinger tendencies. She is made to feel that he can be relied upon to be independent and comforting and that he is not going to be demanding. This means no big flaps if she's late for a tryst and a 'see you around' attitude when they part. It will come as a pleasant change from the Clinger's anxious 'So I'll ring you when you get home to check you arrived safely?' or his 'Where were you? I was beginning to think I'd got the wrong place' (when she's only ten minutes late).

DONOR AND LITTLE PRINCESS

Position in league: **Sixteenth**
Estimated proportion of this type of couple that has
   affairs: **60%**
Most likely unfaithful: **Little Princess**
Most likely third party: **Big Boy Snatcher**

Case history

Keith, the faithful Donor
Lauren, the unfaithful Little Princess
Paul, the third-party Big Boy

Lauren and Keith were the beautiful people. They looked so well together, almost like twins with their fair, wavy hair, slim figures and delicate colouring. And they'd been together for so long that the harmony between them seemed quite natural and effortless. Their friends agreed that it was a pleasure to be with them. The great thing was that you never felt like a gooseberry with them; you always felt 'included'. Everyone always said that if there was one couple that would really stay together for all time, it was Lauren and Keith – they were made for each other.

Lauren loved their peaceful life together, their pretty flat and Keith's gentle, unworldly ways. But there were occasions – and she and Keith often joked about this – when she had what they called her *Wuthering Heights* fantasy: she, a frail, romantic heroine, would be swept off her feet by a swarthy, passionate stranger. Although they enjoyed giggling about this, there were times, darker times, that Keith did not know about, when Lauren felt sadly that life was passing her by, that there was something not right about being with a man who virtually encouraged her to dream about other men.

When the couple met Paul one night it was Keith rather than Lauren who was initially drawn to him. 'A bit Heathcliff, don't you think?' he joked in bed that night. Lauren just smiled and rolled over to go to sleep. But she looked more closely at Paul the next time they met and was not displeased when Keith suggested they all go for a drink. Soon they were meeting often, fast becoming quite a threesome. Lauren enjoyed their times together, the attention of two attractive men, and saw no harm in it. The only discordant note was Keith's probing questioning: had Cathy found her Heathcliff at last? It was hard to imagine Paul asking a girlfriend of his a question like that.

Paul and Lauren are married now. Their friends were incredulous when they heard that Lauren and Keith were splitting up. But Keith says it was in the stars; he couldn't stand in the way of true love. All three have remained the closest of friends. As Paul says, 'Keith played Cupid for us. We really owe him our happiness.'

Profile

The crucial determinant of the couple's happiness is what sort of Little Princess she is. He may go to extreme lengths to prove to himself and her that she would be better with someone else, to express his feelings of unworthiness and inadequacy. He may foster affairs between her and other men.

Some Little Princesses don't want to have affairs. Some are diffident and will ignore the Donor's 'generosity'. Others are under-cover adventuresses and take great care to be discreet. But generally Little Princesses do not like being encouraged to have affairs. They like to hang on to their men – affairs create instability. The key, therefore, is what sort of Little Princess she is.

At its most vulnerable the couple looks like this:

	Partner 1	*Partner 2*
Sexual personality type	Donor	Little Princess
Second tendency	Wimp	Splitter
Third tendency	Bully	Bully

It's not very hard for the Donor to ease affairs along – collapsing into sleep from drunkenness when it's obvious she fancies someone else, not asking her where she got to last night and so on.

They don't get along too well anyway. In bed they are both passive, bored even. She's not getting on with him out of bed either. Neither likes open rows, but there's tension beneath the surface. They don't violently disagree; she sullenly turns her back rather than attacking him directly. They can't talk things out. It's at this point that the Snatcher will succeed if he suggests she move in with him.

At their least vulnerable the partners face stalemate:

	Partner 1	Partner 2
Sexual personality type	Donor	Little Princess
Second tendency	Big Boy	Clinger
Third tendency	Clinger	Splitter

They cling together, yet he keeps putting her in compromising positions with other men. They talk about their problems: he doesn't feel content. Children may help the couple to settle down – but their incompatibility may re-emerge years later.

A Snatcher with Big Boy tendencies will be able to take advantage of the situation if she's been abandoned by her existing partner and needs someone's support. She is in need of reassurance and ripe for a dominant partner who will understand her yearning for both strength and love that does not cloy.

CLINGER AND WIMP

Position in league: **Seventeenth**
Estimated proportion of this type of couple that has affairs: **60%**
Most likely unfaithful: **Wimp**
Most likely third party: **Snatcher with Cosmo or Bully tendencies**

Case history

Sandra, the faithful Clinger
John, the unfaithful Wimp
Cathy, the third-party Cosmo/Snatcher

John and Sandra have lived together for four years. Frankly, Sandra would like to get married, but John thinks marriage is an outmoded institution that degrades women, and Sandra is too afraid of losing him to press the point. John is a poet, very sensitive and original. Sandra has a job in the Civil Service that supports them both. Sandra's widowed mother thinks John is a layabout and a parasite and believes that Sandra should find herself a real man. But Sandra is literally terrified of being on her own. Even when John is away for one night Sandra cannot sleep. The idea of his leaving her for good is too frightening for her to think about. She knows too that in the years that they have been together she has let herself go – lost her figure, drifted out of touch with her old circle of friends. So that now, were she to find herself single again, her chances of getting another man would be very slight.

John is a good man. He genuinely cares for Sandra, and he respects and appreciates her loyalty to him. 'She's the salt of the earth, old Sandra. One of the best. Where would I be without her?' is how he expresses it after several pints with friends at the local. It was in such a mood as this that he wrote the poem that Sandra treasures in which he describes her as his 'anchor, his haven, his earth mother', allowing him, 'the swallow', to scale new heights, secure in the knowledge that she will wait for him. But there are other poems, poems that Sandra will never see because John knows they would destroy her, and even in his bleakest moments of frustration he has never wanted to hurt her. In these Sandra is pictured as the ivy clinging to the nearest object, regardless of whether it be human or rock, and covering it in foliage until it is indistinct from the rest of the landscape, 'just another wave in a sea of mediocrity'.

John knows too that Sandra must never know about Cathy. She is the beautiful, 19-year-old English literature student whom John met six months ago in Leicester after a poetry reading. She came up to him afterwards to discuss his work, and John instantly felt a tremor of passion he had not felt in years with Sandra. Making love with her that night at her bedsit, John felt a sense of freedom that almost made him cry. He knew even then that he could never leave Sandra; he knew also that Cathy, for all her youth and sensitivity, was far too ambitious to shackle herself with somebody like him.

That is the past, a beautiful memory he will carry with him to the grave. Now he must address himself to the future. Sandra is having their baby. He must take care of her now – maybe even get a job and try to abandon once and for all the dream of being an artist.

Profile

This Clinger has found a partner who is reliable if independent, and that makes her less vulnerable to irrational fears of abandonment. However, when she does get nervy and clings he feels suffocated. Wimps prize their freedom highly and find a clinging partner an obstacle to it.

Whereas she enjoys his easygoing, relaxing nature, he wants someone more decisive, more intriguing, than she is.

One consequence can be a shift. Either she develops Cosmo tendencies that make her more appealing despite her clinging, or he finds himself becoming more of a Big Boy. But both of these shifts are rare because clinging and Cosmo tendencies contradict each other. An irrational fear of abandonment and a desire to be independent do not go together. Likewise it's rare for a Wimp to develop a more aggressive style. Sometimes Wimps have Big Boy values or sexual identities and still remain Wimps but that's unusual.

It is more likely that the Wimp will become open to the idea of an affair without actively seeking one. It's a question of the right third party making the first move at the right time. A Snatcher of any tendency can succeed if she picks the right moment, but she'll have to initiate the affair. She's unlikely to have Clinger tendencies (unless he has a thing about Clingers) and most likely to have assertive Cosmo leanings with which she persuades him he's been with the wrong woman; a Bully who conceals her rejecting, angry side can be similarly convincing that she's the one for him.

Stable, faithful Clinger–Wimp couples are usually a variation of the following theme:

	Partner 1	Partner 2
Sexual personality type	Clinger	Wimp
Second tendency	Cosmo	Clinger
Third tendency	Splitter	Donor

The key elements are that the potentially unfaithful is, in fact, a Donor on the lust dimension and therefore not prone to affairs and that he is quite a Clinger too, so he has quite a need for her. For her part, a Cosmo tendency provides the kind of woman he most wants. These two can form a quiet, relatively compatible unit that satisfies both enough to ensure that they don't succumb to roaming Snatchers. This combination is close, private and hard to penetrate.

By contrast, in the most vulnerable case the Wimp is like a ripe fruit waiting to be plucked:

	Partner 1	Partner 2
Sexual personality type	Clinger	Wimp
Second tendency	Little Princess	Splitter
Third tendency	Donor	Bully

Alongside the suffocation of her clinging, The Wimp finds her Little Princess values and sexual attitudes obnoxious. His Splitter tendencies make him very open to a Snatcher Cosmo or, if she succeeds in masquerading as a Cosmo, a Snatcher Bully. To the extent that the Clinger's Donor tendency is strong, the Snatcher's task will be that much easier. The situation is pregnant with risk, and the scene is set for a classic 'I don't know what came over me' scenario. He is alone with a Snatcher Cosmo: 'It just happened.'

WIMP AND LITTLE PRINCESS

Position in league: **Eighteenth**
Estimated proportion of this type of couple that has
   affairs: **58%**
Most likely unfaithful: **The partner with a Splitter
second tendency**
Most likely third party: **Someone who is compatible on
the dominance dimension**

Case history

Ray, the faithful Wimp
Janet, the unfaithful Little Princess
Terry, the third-party Big Boy

Ray and Janet already knew each other quite well when they
started going out together. They both worked as technicians
in the film industry, had many mutual friends and had often
worked side by side on projects. After a late night at the pub
they were both surprised when they found themselves going
home together and in bed both found the combination of
familiarity and shyness stimulating. They were surprised to
find themselves being so passionate with someone they knew
well. It seemed a good idea to continue the relationship. It
had never previously occurred to either that friendship and
shared interests could be a good basis for an affair: both
had always unthinkingly worked on the 'opposites attract'
principle.

   After a few months a change of circumstance made it
convenient for Janet to move in with Ray. It seemed sensible,
since they spent most nights together anyway, and they
agreed that if it didn't work, they would call it a day and no
hard feelings.

   It was quite soon after this that things began to go wrong –
not dramatically (they didn't row) but both sensed a change.

For a start, the sparkle went out of their sex life. Both were always tired after work and unromantic after an evening spent cooking the supper and watching TV. Both secretly felt that if the other initiated things they would be willing, but couldn't be bothered themselves. And that spontaneous mutual lust that had been such an unexpected joy at first seemed to have vanished into thin air. Perhaps it was awkwardness caused by their shared celibacy, and their own natural passivity, that stopped them talking too. Anyway they both realized they had a bad situation on their hands, but neither seemed able to do anything about it.

Terry was a godsend. When he first started showing an interest in Janet she played it cool but secretly felt really excited. He seemed so sure of what he wanted, and he wanted her.

Ray did not react suspiciously to the lame excuses that Janet made when she was going out to meet Terry. She barely felt guilty. Not long afterwards she moved out. She doesn't know how things will work out with Terry, but the pleasurable anxiety she feels about him leaves no room for thoughts of Ray. He doesn't seem that bothered either. He's more interested in his work and in the new girl working in the wardrobe department. Janet and Ray haven't managed to remain friends, though neither can explain what went wrong between them.

Profile

Both partners are reasonable people who may well love each other dearly for good reasons. And yet there will always be a basic feeling that somehow they're not right together, an uncomfortable itch that just won't go away.

In bed, for example, it only works initially. They may find each other a contrast to forceful partners they have known. The problems come after a few weeks. A tentativeness creeps into their lovemaking. They sense each other's desire but, the early excitement having worn off, neither naturally makes the first move. They don't talk about it. It's in neither's nature to instigate such a talk. They feel dissatisfied, and each blames the other. From now on they are vulnerable to affairs. Which one of them actually has an affair depends on the combination of other tendencies.

At its most vulnerable, the couple sinks rapidly into a state of apathy:

	Partner 1	Partner 2
Sexual personality type	Wimp	Little Princess
Second tendency	Splitter – either partner	
Third tendency	Bully	Bully

If it's the Wimp who has the Splitter second tendency, any self-respecting Cosmo who wants him will succeed. She'll be the decisive, thrilling, 'fascinating' woman he's missed in his current partner. He hasn't been able to see eye to eye with his Little Princess on values: she believes he should be more of a macho man, wants to feel he's in charge, wants *in*equality in their relationship. With a Cosmo he finds at last a woman who wants to be equal, to take it in turns – although she's the dominant figure.

Likewise the Little Princess. A Big Boy and she will suddenly hit it off, and she'll realize *this* is what she really wants. In place of the Wimp's indecisiveness and equivocation comes a real man's dominance. He wants to pay for the meals, to walk her home, to shepherd and cosset her.

In this most vulnerable version, the Splitter is the one whose fancy starts to wander. At the same time, they have rows sparked by a shared Bully third tendency. These may be low-key to an observer – awkward silences, bitchy comments, backbiting to friends. She may make jokes about his lack of sexual mastery or even potency. He grimaces, and she regrets saying these things afterwards but, deep down, feels they are true.

The couple is least vulnerable when one or other veers towards a different personality type:

	Partner 1	*Partner 2*
Sexual personality type	Wimp	Little Princess
Second tendency	Bully/Clinger	Clinger/Bully
Third tendency	Splitter/Donor	Donor/Splitter

If the Little Princess has some Cosmo in her and the Wimp has some Big Boy tendencies, they may get along. If one of them changes altogether, the partnership will actually work well. The Bully–Clinger contrast also helps. When angry, the Bully provides the dominance and urgency that they badly need from one of them if the relationship is to last.

SPLITTER AND BULLY

Position in league: **Nineteenth**
Estimated proportion of this type of couple that has
   affairs: **58%**
Most likely unfaithful: **Splitter**
Most likely third party: **A Snatcher who is compatible on the dominance dimension**

Case history

Francis, the faithful Bully
Cheryl, the unfaithful Splitter
Simon, the third-party Big Boy

Cheryl's father had always had a terrible temper. He didn't actually hit her often, but he could be fearsome when enraged. She now thinks that had a big effect on her.

Cheryl: 'Dad was a big man, and so is Francis. Dad used to control us with a rod of iron. So does Francis. Dad was always very open about sex and would tell me how I was *his* little girl. Likewise Francis. Now, I think that's what attracted me, Francis being like my Dad.

'We've always had a pattern to our sex life, Francis and I. He'll lose his temper over some minor matter and start to shout at me. I'll say I'm sorry – the worst thing I could do would be to argue back. Then suddenly it all changes. It's as though he's got something out of his system. In the peace that follows he'll grab me. Suddenly he wants me rather than hates me.

'We'd only been married, what? four years when I met Simon. I've never known Simon lose his temper. He's very assertive, but he doesn't get angry at all. He's charming and he's a big, strong man who knows what he wants.

'At first he paid me no attention to speak of. I was just one of a number of people he'd run into every so often at the pub. But one evening he came over and chatted to me when I was out with a couple of girlfriends. This happened several times in the next few weeks, and it was pretty obvious he fancied me. I fancied him too, but the idea of doing anything made my blood run cold – what Francis would do if he ever saw another man paying me attention wasn't worth thinking about.

'Around this time I was getting more and more fed up with Francis's moods. One night I stormed out of the house and went to the pub on my own. As soon as Simon saw me alone he came over. He was very understanding and bought me a few drinks. Eventually he offered me a lift home and asked me in for a coffee on the way. When I got up to leave he kissed me goodbye. I vowed not to see him again. But there was a next time and a time after that . . .'

Francis: 'I knew she was having an affair because she was getting very troublesome. She'd shout at me and tell me to "do it yourself" when I tried to get her to be more efficient in running the house. She's *so* incompetent. One evening she set off for a "girls' night" at the Prince of Wales. I decided to follow her. I stood outside in the rain, looking into the warmth of the lounge, and what I saw made me see red. She was canoodling with a man, the little slut!

'I was so angry I was in total control. It was raining cats and dogs, but I didn't care. About an hour before closing time they came out. They went in his car to a flat not far from here.

I waited until they'd had five minutes or so then I climbed in a back window.

'I lost my rag. If he'd been a smaller man, he'd be dead now. I hit him with flailing fists. He won't do it again. Nor will she, or next time I swear she'll be the one who gets it.'

Cheryl: 'Francis thinks that just because he beat up Simon he's proved his point. That's what I love about Francis – he's very straightforward. He'll fight for what he's got, and what he's got is me. But though he would never admit it, I think he's changed since then. He controls his temper and tries to make me feel wanted. After my affair with Simon he was furious, but we soon made it up.'

Profile

This relationship gets ugly at the drop of a hat and, even if there is fidelity, is never peaceable. The Bully is always prone to paranoia in general and to expecting to be taken for a ride by partners in particular. Put him with a Splitter and there's good reason to be nervous: the Splitter's eye is for ever wandering. On top of this, being bullied does not encourage fidelity and if the Splitter isn't a Little Princess, the irrational outbursts, accusations and rages only serve to push her away.

Even where there is compatibility on the dominance dimension (Wimp–Cosmo, Little Princess–Big Boy), it's never going to be easy: boat-rocking from both sides means there's always an undercurrent of bad temper.

The sex isn't going to work brilliantly after the first few months either. The Splitter's desire wanes inevitably, and whether there are affairs or not the best that can happen is a sort of sullen stalemate.

At its most vulnerable the couple looks like this:

	Partner 1	*Partner 2*
Sexual personality type	Splitter	Bully
Second tendency	Bully	Donor
Third tendency	Incompatibility on the dominance dimension	

Clashes over lateness, whose turn it is to do the washing up and so on build up rapidly. The rejection each experiences, *regardless of what actually happens*, creates running sores. Both imagine they are being exploited. Both feel that their needs are being ignored. And so on, except that one of them has a weapon the other does not have: the Splitter takes revenge through affairs.

These affairs cause bitter acrimony. Rage boils up in the Bully, yet his Donor second tendency helps to promote the affairs, as do depression and his sense of unworthiness. It's sheer agony for the Bully, who is torn between breaking off the relationship altogether and watching his partner's antics with fascination.

In the end a Snatcher cleans up. The Splitter needs little persuading that happiness lies elsewhere. The Bully is absolutely furious and may fight like mad to hang on but eventually will probably lose his partner.

The least vulnerable version of this couple is not much better:

	Partner 1	Partner 2
Sexual personality type	Splitter	Bully
Second tendency	Compatibility on the dominance dimension	
Third tendency	Clinger	Donor

While compatible dominance creates a basis for love, instability always threatens. At its simplest, the Bully drives the Splitter crazy with his constant criticism and bad temper and she becomes vulnerable to offers from third parties. However, if they're lucky, no Snatcher comes along or no suitable opportunity presents itself for the Snatcher to strike.

CLINGER AND CLINGER

Position in league: **Twentieth**
Estimated proportion of this type of couple that has
  affairs: **52%**
Most likely unfaithful: **Wimp**
Most likely third party: **Snatcher with dominant
  tendencies (Big Boy, Cosmo or Bully)**

Case history

Heather, the faithful Clinger
Patrick, the unfaithful Clinger
Janie, the third-party Snatcher

Patrick and Heather met while studying marine biology at
university. They always said it was love at first sight. Both
had been unhappy in childhood. Heather's family lived
under the shadow of her father's unpredictable, violent
temper, which, even after she had left home, caused her to
live in a state of constant timidity. Patrick, on the other hand,
came from an apparently cheerful home, yet he always felt
inadequate and dull by comparison with his attractive,
bubbly older sister and his studious but popular younger
brother. Both had had love affairs long before Patrick, and he
was beginning to feel that he had missed the boat. So when he
met Heather he felt not just desire but also gratitude to her for
returning his feelings. Patrick was not Heather's first boyfriend. She had had a number of relationships, but they had
all ended disastrously when she began to accuse her partner
of not taking the affair as seriously as she did.

  She could have no complaints about Patrick on this score.
From the very outset his commitment to Heather was pro-
found. They quickly became inseparable. No one was surprised when, shortly after graduation, they announced their
intention of marrying.

That was twelve years ago. Since then they have lived quietly in a detached house in a suburb of a small university town. Both teach at the local grammar school and meet frequently during the day – in fact, they are rarely apart for more than a few hours at a time. Sadly, early on in their marriage Heather discovered she was unable to bear children, and their sex life, which had never been very dynamic, came to a complete halt not long after. But they have been content after their fashion.

It is only very recently that Patrick has begun to question their happiness. For Heather, even now, every day without violence of some sort is like balm to the scars of her childhood. When she sees the misery that her mother still lives in she feels fortunate beyond her wildest dreams. She still sometimes has nightmares about losing Patrick. But when Patrick looks around he sees something different. He sees the bright, lively – if erratic – lives that his brother and sister have made for themselves; he looks at his own neat, orderly existence, and he sees a poor thing. Perhaps he was too hasty in settling down. He forgets now the loneliness and insecurity he felt before he met Heather and remembers only the dexterity with which she bound him to her, with her hard-luck stories and her dog-like adoration.

Patrick has only ever slept with one woman, and not with her for several years. He begins to have sexual fantasies, and increasingly they centre on Janie, a young single parent of two who has recently moved to their neighbourhood. He does not know whether he will ever act on any of these fantasies, for he knows that were Heather to suspect that his eye was straying, it would precipitate something akin to a nervous breakdown in her. He feels that his is an almost hopeless predicament.

Profile

Like the Babes in the Wood, these two cling to each other for dear life, and this can be a solution to their problems. Both fear abandonment, so both constantly try to reassure themselves that the other is going to stay for ever. Neither is very prone to affairs. Their relationship can be a stable stalemate that lasts for years.

On the other hand, insecurity can make the couple a tense and fearful one. A cycle of clinging can bring them so close together that their need for each other becomes pathological. They are unable to act independently. Even going to work becomes a major trauma for both; they can't bear to be apart.

However, the less insecure of the two may begin to feel more confident and to shift towards a new personality type. The other will try to maintain the status quo, but if he or she fails, the partner with the new personality type will start fighting for freedom.

Since neither is secure enough to enjoy sex much in its own right, their sexual relationship is patchy and not an important feature of their life. This means that if one of them has, or develops, strong Splitter tendencies, he or she will become particularly dissatisfied and will be very open to offers. As Clingers neither is likely to initiate an affair, but they are willing recipients of interest shown by suitable third parties.

The couples among whom infidelity overrides the mutual clinging tend to look like this:

	Partner 1	Partner 2
Sexual personality type	Clinger	Clinger
Second tendency	Donor	Splitter
Third tendency	Wimp/Little Princess	

If the Little Princess is the Splitter, then she's seduced away from her partner by a snatching, dominant Big Boy. Classically, she is attractive but shy, and he brings her to life. She feels he has woken her from a long sleep. Looking back on all that time with her Clinger–Wimp, she suddenly realizes how insular and suffocated she felt. That she will soon start suffocating the Big Boy quickly becomes apparent, and he may drop her when she starts getting demanding. Rightly, as it happens, she fears abandonment by him – even though her fear is irrational. It is the cause of precisely the event she worries about most.

If it's the Wimp who is the Splitter, he's 'liberated' by a Cosmo. She shows him the joys of sex with an active woman. He too looks back on his Clinger–Little Princess as someone who stifled him. But his Cosmo likes her independence, and this brings out his insecurity before long. Clingers who have affairs are prone to losing their nerve and, if paired with another Clinger, instead of changing partner often just have a fling before returning to first base – where they are welcomed with open arms.

However, this combination is incompatible on the dominance dimension – Wimps and Little Princesses don't see eye to eye; if the second tendencies are Big Boy and Cosmo, it's almost as bad, and their strong Donor–Splitter tendencies produce regular Donor–Splitter cycles. They lurch from affairs to tearful reunions, to a claustrophobically intense and insular relationship and back into yet another affair. Eventually they either accept an open relationship or the Splitter forgoes sex rather than have all the grief involved in the Donor–Splitter cycle.

At the opposite extreme is a relatively stable and faithful combination:

	Partner 1	Partner 2
Sexual personality type	Clinger	Clinger
Second tendency	Big Boy	Little Princess
Third tendency	Donor	Splitter

Here compatibility on the dominance dimension means that they can cling together without becoming claustrophobic. At least they share values and sexual identity, and they don't clash in their styles of aggression. The lust factor is unlikely to endanger them: their sex life may not be very exciting, but it doesn't collapse altogether. It would take a highly persistent and very skilful Snatcher to break into their private and cordoned-off life together. These two don't expect too much out of life and settle for what they've got, limited though it is.

BULLY AND WIMP

Position in league: **Twenty-first**
Estimated proportion of this type of couple that has
    affairs: **50%**
Most likely unfaithful: **Wimp**
Most likely third party: **Cosmo**

Case history

Sam, the faithful Wimp
Kate, the unfaithful Bully
George, the third-party Clinger

Sam's quiet, meditative approach to life had begun to annoy Kate. She felt unappreciated. He'd done A-levels and trained as a lawyer, and she wasn't stupid either, but to judge by the way he reacted to things she said – he offered little or no response – she felt he thought he was superior. Bully Kate saw rejection in what was really only Wimpishness. 'And the way he'd behave at parties – as if we were quite separate. He seemed almost to encourage me to go off with other men just by his lack of observation. Was he blind or something?' No, he had a Donor second tendency.

Sam: 'I found myself withdrawing when she got into her moods. Temper tantrums, raging furies – I've never seen the like. It was horrific. And the quieter I became, the more it stoked the fire. It would get to the point where I would wish she'd shove off, go with someone else even, just stop stamping on me. I like forceful women, but I draw the line at one who kicks me. She used literally to start kicking.' Occasionally Sam's bullying third tendency would take over and he'd kick back.

It was soon after one such incident that Kate met George. 'I was feeling low. I wanted someone who'd appreciate me, my looks, my mind – someone who didn't lash out at me. George, in fact. I used to go into a café at lunchtimes. I struck up a conversation with him. He seemed vulnerable and it brought out my caring side to see him serving coffee – hot, over-worked, underpaid. We used to talk a lot. Once he could see I wanted him he was *very* responsive, not like Sam.' Clinger George found her domineering ways to his taste, and the Wimp in him suited her Cosmo side. A real love affair blossomed. Something like adoration arose between them. For three months it remained a secret. Then Kate told Sam. He was (to her) surprisingly upset. The triangle dragged on for nearly a year until eventually Sam realized that Kate and he would be far better off apart. 'Part of me knew I should leave [his Wimp self], but another part kept me locked into the situation. It was perverse almost, my refusal to see the writing on the wall sooner.' In fact, he was unsuited to Kate, and she was far better suited to her new lover. The way it turned out was best for all concerned.

Profile

This Wimp almost certainly confuses the Bully with a Cosmo. He mistakes her insistence and aggression for force-ful assertiveness. What at first seemed attractive to him eventually seems rather different. Her worst moods are awesome to behold; she is routinely prickly, stroppy and critical. While he's a tolerant sort of bloke, he's also realistic, and there comes a time when he realizes he's involved with a woman who has got problems. If he's got Splitter tendencies, this is when he begins to wander.

However, if it's the Bully that's the Splitter, she may wander. She will have grievances that have little substance and, despite their lack of foundation, she will want to take revenge. Affairs may be one method she'll use. But unless she's a pronounced Splitter, chances are that it'll be he and not she who feels in need of a new relationship.

And it is a different *relationship* that he seeks, not just sex. She keeps on at him about things ('Why are you always late?') or she persistently lets him down (by being terminally late herself). She makes him feel very uncomfortable because she can't leave things alone when she is irritated. She'll lie there last thing at night, picking the scab, making the wound worse long after it's obvious that there's nothing more to be said and he's very sleepy: 'But if you had to work late, how come your secretary did too? It's a bit of a coincidence'; 'You say you love me and then you go and arrange for us to be apart. I know you can't help it if your boss sends you away, but I bet you wouldn't go if you really loved me'; and so on.

At its least vulnerable, however, the couple's relationship is not necessarily like this for much of the time:

	Partner 1	Partner 2
Sexual personality type	Bully	Wimp
Second tendency	Cosmo	Clinger
Third tendency	Splitter	Donor

It helps if the Bully's rejecting anger is reduced by the stability of the Wimp. Her sense of grievance runs up against the fact that he's reliable, tolerant and understanding. After a bit she may notice that she's being irrational – he doesn't want to hurt her or to reject her. Although she continues to have the outbursts, at times (usually with hindsight) she can see they are unreasonable. Gradually this insight and his stability help her to be less of a Bully and more of the confident, healthily assertive Cosmo that he wants.

At the same time this couple are helped by his clinging second tendency which makes him more resolute in his attempts to see it through. He's prepared to sacrifice a lot to get her to change because he doesn't want to lose her.

It takes a very wily Snatcher to break them up because they're learning from each other and finding it rewarding. However, a Wimp Snatcher who catches the Bully alone and in one of her moods may be able to turn her irrational anger towards her partner to advantage. She's likely to have had a few drinks, and in the morning she'll be full of remorse because in this variation the Bully and her regular partner probably do love each other.

At its most vulnerable the combination is as follows:

	Partner 1	Partner 2
Sexual personality type	Bully	Wimp
Second tendency	Little Princess	Splitter
Third tendency	Donor	Bully

She gets at him sometimes in the most wounding of ways. She says things that can never be forgiven. As she is a Little Princess and he a Wimp, she may attack his masculinity and his values. She picks on his areas of greatest self-doubt and plunges a spear into them.

The sex is never very satisfactory and rapidly collapses. His Bully side means that he also gets angry sometimes and even in bed they find all sorts of roundabout ways of attacking each other. And it's only a matter of time before he uses sex as the way out. He is sexually frustrated, but it's the new *relationship* that comes as such a relief when finally he leaves her and takes up with a Cosmo. The affair may be short-lived, however, for this reason: he fell quickly for his new partner because of the contrast with the Bully.

For her part, the Bully in this couple is always enraged by his departure and offers it as proof (to anyone who'll listen) that her complaints about him were justified. She rants and raves and may avenge herself if she can find a way. If there's a divorce, it'll be a nasty one.

BULLY AND LITTLE PRINCESS

Position in league: **Twenty-second**
Estimated proportion of this type of couple that has affairs: **50%**
Most likely unfaithful: **Little Princess**
Most likely third party: **Big Boy**

Case history

Samantha, the faithful Little Princess
Dick, the unfaithful Bully
Jill, the third-party Little Princess

This is a typical tale of 'older woman loses out to younger woman', but the cause is more subtle than the simple fact that the latter is much prettier than the former.

Samantha was feeling her age: 'I remember going shopping and thinking that a particular dress wasn't for me any more, that my legs and waist wouldn't survive it and I'd look like mutton dressed up as lamb. I remember trying on a very cute patterned dress and catching myself in the mirror. It was awful – I looked like an old hag. That was only occasionally though, just the usual growing pains.' She also found herself sometimes comparing herself adversely with other women. At the same time she was finding Dick's less pleasant side – which had always been there – harder to take. 'One night he spoilt a whole evening. He got very tipsy and was so dogmatic and so angry that the evening broke up early. Our friends were really embarrassed by it.'

Dick can recall that evening too: 'Yes, I vaguely remember. Some berk was talking absolute codswallop, and the next morning I was a bit hung-over. She was sitting there looking like something the cat brought in, and I was thinking, "Why am I married to that?" when she started on at me about the previous night. She had the gall to say I'd been foolish and embarrassing!' Very much a Bully's-eye view of the incident.

Meanwhile, about this time at the office Dick found himself in the company of a young and attractive fellow employee, Jill. She contrived a number of incidents designed to trap him but found him a difficult man to snatch. As he puts it, 'I'm not highly sexed; I know what I like and I believe in loyalty.' However, patience and persistence mixed with a certain coyness of demeanour eventually led him to the point where they were routinely exchanging the odd kiss but always holding back. In the end Jill needed Samantha's

Donor tendency to tip the scales in her favour. At a colleague's party Samantha felt so dispirited by what she saw as her lack of attractiveness that she not only left early but insisted that Dick stay on even though he was ready to go. Jill took her chance with courage and aplomb, and Dick succumbed.

The triangle still continues because Jill cannot quite prise Dick away from his wife altogether – he is not quite motivated enough by desire – while Samantha is unable to put her foot down and issue an ultimatum. It's a situation that is causing much angst and giving little satisfaction.

Profile

This Little Princess made a mistake. She thought that the Bully's aggression was forceful assertiveness. His 'positive' qualities vanished early on: now he is generally bad-tempered and difficult to please. She's fairly easy-going, but she has a good head on her shoulders and realizes that her man is nothing but trouble. If she's got Splitter tendencies, this is when she begins to wander.

It's the fact that they don't get on together which is at the core of her discontent. He criticizes her constantly – though he is by no means perfect himself.

At their least vulnerable, however, the partners may get along some of the time:

	Partner 1	Partner 2
Sexual personality type	Bully	Little Princess
Second tendency	Big Boy	Clinger
Third tendency	Splitter	Donor

The Bully's anger may be deflected by the stability of the Little Princess. She is blatantly not the cause of his problems. Although he's not always in control of his temper, he begins to see that his tantrums are irrational. Gradually he learns to be less of a Bully.

This couple is supported by the Clinger in her, which

makes her prepared to stand by him through thick and thin. Her Clinger fear is that he'll abandon her.

A canny Little Princess Snatcher may be able to lure him away from his partner. He'll regret it, though: deep down, he loves his own Princess.

At its most vulnerable the combination is as follows:

	Partner 1	Partner 2
Sexual personality type	Bully	Little Princess
Second tendency	Wimp	Splitter
Third tendency	Donor	Bully

He wounds her by saying things that she will never forgive or forget. He attacks exactly where he will do the most damage: her confidence ('I suppose you call yourself an adult. So why can't you act like one?'). She retaliates on occasion (she has a Bully third tendency, after all), but eventually she will seek solace elsewhere.

The new *relationship* with a Big Boy is exhilarating. But it doesn't last long: it is based on her desire to escape. And the Bully is maddened by her defection. It is proof that he was right about her all along. She was never reliable – considered only her own needs and desires. He's been had, and she'll pay. She would be wise to keep out of his way: he will make trouble for her if he can, especially if it comes to a divorce.

CLINGER AND DONOR

Position in league: **Twenty-third**
Estimated proportion of this type of couple that has
    affairs: **46%**
Most likely unfaithful: **Clinger**
Most likely third party: **Clinger with compatibility on the dominance dimension**

Case history

Jeremy, the faithful Clinger
Kate, the unfaithful Donor
Cheryl, the third-party Clinger

The events that occurred last summer when Jeremy and Kate were on holiday would have been amusing if they hadn't been harrowing. Jeremy is a handsome, youthful 35-year-old; his wife Kate is two years older, less good-looking but with a good brain and a wicked sense of humour that win her many friends. They are a successful, hard-working couple with two bright children. It was with the intention of spending some time with their children that they took a villa in Greece for a month last summer. Cheryl, the 18-year-old daughter of friends, came with them to help with the children and the cooking.

The trouble started when Kate thought she saw Jeremy eyeing Cheryl in her bikini and made some joke about it. Jeremy responded in kind and thought no more of it. The next day Kate brought the matter up again, this time adding, 'And I think she's got a crush on you.'

'Don't be ridiculous, darling. I'm old enough to be her father,' answered Jeremy, slightly irritably. 'And anyway what if she does? You know I never look at other women. I'm famous for it!'

This in turn nettled Kate: 'Well, you needn't be so smug about it. I think an affair would do you good. You've been with me since you were practically a schoolboy. Now, don't tell me you aren't at least a little curious . . .'

The conversation was abruptly ended by the entrance of Cheryl herself. Jeremy did not even glance at her tanned, lean young body in its skimpy bikini as he left the room.

But in bed that night Kate insisted on bringing the matter up again. 'Look, take it from me, Jem, that girl has got the hots for you. And in my opinion it would do neither of you any harm to act on it. I could take the children off for a few days. I think the change would do us all good.'

Jeremy was beginning to get annoyed in earnest: 'What the hell are you talking about? Have you heard yourself? I love you and only you. The idea of having an adolescent fling with a schoolgirl just isn't my scene. I want to be unfaithful about as little as I want you to be unfaithful to me. How would you feel if I started talking like that? Honestly it makes me wonder how much you really love me.'

And so it continued, getting more and more out of hand – until Jeremy began to suspect that Kate herself was having an affair and was trying to get rid of him.

By the end of the summer, when they returned to London, their nerves were quite frayed. Yet when Jeremy told his friend Bob of the tense situation that had developed in Greece, Bob laughed uproariously. 'You two are ludicrous,' he said. 'God, I should have your luck.' But Jeremy just shook his head sadly. He still can't work out why Kate seemed so eager for him to betray her, and it worries him.

Profile

This can be a strange couple because two opposed forces are pulling in different directions and producing distortions in the way each sees the other. The Donor routinely sets up the Clinger to go off with other partners; the Clinger experiences this as abandonment, which is not the intention, so clings ever harder. The more the Donor offers escape, the harder the Clinger clings. Power in the couple ends up mostly with the Donor as a result. Ironically, the last thing the Donor feels is powerful, attractive or important.

At its most vulnerable the couple looks like this:

	Partner 1	Partner 2
Sexual personality type	Clinger	Donor
Second tendency	Splitter	Dominance-incompatible
Third tendency	Dominance-incompatible	Bully

This is bizarre. There is not only a conflict between the Clinger and the Donor but, in addition, a conflict within the Clinger. He is for ever yearning for an affair with a third party who is up for it, yet the Clinger in him says, 'Don't do it. You'll end up with no one.'

The result is chaos all round. The Donor does nothing to help because she is unwittingly making matters worse by encouraging affairs. On top of this there is their incompatibility on the dominance dimension. If they're both laid-back, passive types (most common in this variation), the relationship drifts like a rudderless ship without a captain. If they're both dominant types (Cosmo and Big Boy), overt disagreements spring up, and the confusion of their position makes the Donor particularly angry. The Clinger feels angry too but daren't express it.

At its least vulnerable the relationship is still messy:

	Partner 1	Partner 2
Sexual personality type	Clinger	Donor
Second tendency	Dominance-compatible	Clinger
Third tendency	Splitter	Dominance-compatible

While infidelity is rare in this permutation, it's more of a stalemate than a winning recipe. The basic conflict of Donor and Clinger governs much of what transpires between them despite their compatibility. They may get on fine in terms of shared interests, friends and lifestyle, but they will be confused by each other's behaviour at a deep, emotional level. It is a very hard relationship for a Snatcher to penetrate. The snatch is constantly subverted by the Clinger's anxiety. He or she keeps saying, 'I must be off,' just when the Snatcher is making some headway. It's not long before the Snatcher decides to hunt in a different part of the jungle.

CLINGER AND BULLY

Position in league: **Twenty-fourth**
Estimated proportion of this type of couple that has
   affairs: **45%**
Most likely unfaithful: **Bully**
Most likely third party: **Wimp, Cosmo or Clinger**

Case history

Alice, the faithful Clinger
Brian, the unfaithful Bully
Sarah, the third-party Little Princess

Alice's words frequently contradicted her deeds. In theory she felt she should not spend so much time with Brian, should lead her own life, quite distinct from their life together. In practice she tended to end up staying in with him. That suited him fine except that unpredictably, when an upsurge of independence took hold of her, she would leave him alone for an evening, high and dry and without much warning.

When Sarah appeared on the scene she quickly grasped that Brian was vulnerable to the right approach. She mistook his bullying for Big Boy behaviour and, sensing that a snatch could be made, found him increasingly desirable. She didn't expect it to last, but she fancied a fling. The trouble came a few weeks later, when Alice found out. She was furious. At the same time Sarah pulled out; she'd begun to be on the wrong end of his bullying side and to realize he was not all Big Boy. Brian had to crawl back to Alice, burying his pride and shattered at being dropped by Sarah. Brian is showing clear signs of becoming more of a Wimp on the dominance dimension. If this continues he and Alice may turn out to be well matched after all.

Profile

These two are well matched in several respects, their insecurity notwithstanding. The Bully does not interpret the Clinger's incessant demands and displays of concern as rejection. He may sneer, but secretly he rather likes having someone so dependent on him. At times of tension he says things like 'We deserve each other' and in a way he is right. It's easy for Bullies to be reassured that they are needed by Clingers – Bullies' threats of leaving elicit all the conformation they could hope for that they are not in danger of rejection.

However, the Bully needs constant confirmation that the Clinger is not rejecting him. Ludicrous, totally contradictory situations may be created – the Bully desperately trying to force the Clinger to reject him by rocking the boat or by saying, 'You stick to me like a leech, but it proves you don't really care for *me*. It's what I stand for that you cling to. It could be anybody, really, but it just happens to be me.' And this is true, but that's not why the Bully is saying it. He is saying it to try to sting the Clinger into rejecting him so that his expectation can have some basis in fact. In extreme cases the Bully might start having affairs in order to upset the Clinger into rejecting him. It's a complex relationship.

Even if the Bully does resort to affairs, it still may not lead the Clinger to reject him, so great is the terror of abandonment. From the Clinger's standpoint the Bully's domineering, controlling side is reassuring. She would rather someone behaved like that than acted independently or diffidently. Someone who's running your life for you seems less likely to abandon you. Nor does the Clinger find the angry outbursts and irrational attacks too painful. She feels that it shows her partner cares.

The Clinger senses that the Bully is as insecure as she. At times the two of them are very close because they understand each other's terrors intuitively. They may not realize that their fears are not the same, but they feel united by their quirky, anxious way of relating.

However, these periods of closeness are interrupted every

so often because each often misinterprets the other's behaviour. Although rejection could not be farther from the Clinger's mind, and although a wish to abandon the Clinger is hardly the Bully's main concern, each insists on finding evidence for those expectations in the other's behaviour.

Infidelity is unlikely if neither has strong Donor or Splitter tendencies. It is most likely if there is a strong Splitter tendency in the Bully. In such cases sex is likely to break down between them and, blaming the Clinger, the Bully is liable to go off in search of someone who finds him attractive as revenge for imagined criticism of his desirability. A Clinger with strong Splitter tendencies is less likely to seek affairs because she daren't risk losing her partner, but a wily Snatcher who spots the splitting desire may just be able to coax the Clinger into bed. Another cause of affairs is mismatching on the dominance dimension. People with Big Boy and Cosmo personality types as strong second tendencies may find that their personalities lead to clashes that make Little Princesses and Wimps attractive.

Finally, shifts in personality will prompt affairs. If either partner shifts towards a more dominant personality type, this will destroy the original basis of the relationship. The more dominant partner will cease to be so insecure and will become more aware of how irrational the behaviour of their lover is. This will make him or her very open to a compatibly dominant third party. A Bully who becomes a Big Boy, for example, will be looking to trade in his Clinger for a Little Princess; an ex-Bully Cosmo will start to find herself tempted more and more by less demanding and more rational Wimps.

The stable, faithful Clinger–Bully combination always has a compatible pair of second tendencies on the dominance dimension:

	Partner 1	Partner 2
Sexual personality type	Clinger	Bully
Second tendency	Cosmo/Little Princess	Wimp/Big Boy
Third tendency	Splitter	Donor

It's important that the Bully is the one with the Donor tendencies here – splitting Bullies, even when splitting is a third tendency, are volatile and prone to one-night stands. Clingers with a Splitter third tendency rarely act on it – they take a lot of persuasion to have an affair anyway, and only a Snatcher has the persistence to succeed with them. With the lust factor ruled out in this way, compatible second tendencies on the dominance dimension nicely complement the calming effect that the Bully's insecurity has on the Clinger and vice versa. It means they are on the same wavelength sexually and share similar attitudes. And dominant Bullies are fine for submissive Clingers as far as style of aggression goes. This combination is unlikely to be unfaithful because a compatible Clinger-Bully cycle is in operation:

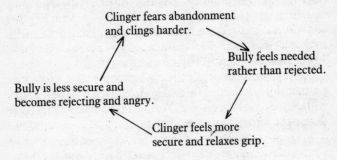

Clinger fears abandonment and clings harder.

Bully feels needed rather than rejected.

Bully is less secure and becomes rejecting and angry.

Clinger feels more secure and relaxes grip.

This cycle is short-circuited in the most vulnerable combination of tendencies:

	Partner 1	Partner 2
Sexual personality type	Clinger	Bully
Second tendency	Cosmo	Splitter
Third tendency	Donor	Big Boy

When the clinging starts here it activates the Bully's splitting tendency. Familiarity dims the sexual attraction, and the Bully seeks third parties. At the same time the Cosmo tendency of the Clinger makes her talk about independence and increases the risk that the Bully will feel rejected. Although the Clinger doesn't act independently in practice, her talking about it makes the Bully angry. In this combination it also clashes with his third-tendency Big Boy values and sexual identity. An act of infidelity becomes almost inevitable.

A similar short-circuiting of the cycle happens if there is a Wimp–Little Princess pairing on the dominance dimension. The clash of types exacerbates an already volatile situation and catapults the Bully into an affair. However, this incompatibility is not as serious as the Big Boy–Cosmo clash, which is always the worst.

The third party need not have strong snatching tendencies. Once the splitting Bully goes on the rampage he has no need for much encouragement.

CLINGER AND COSMO

Position in league: **Twenty-fifth**
Estimated proportion of this type of couple that has
  affairs: **45%**
Most likely unfaithful: **Cosmo**
Most likely third party: **Wimp**

Case history

Ken, the faithful Clinger
Diane, the unfaithful Cosmo
Andy, the third-party Wimp

Diane was a successful career girl in her early thirties when she met Ken. She had her own flat, a car, a super job and a circle of friends that seemed to include more and more married couples with kids. Ken impressed her initially with his hunky good looks, his athleticism and his boisterous enthusiasms. He seemed a far cry from the clever, cynical, cultivated young men she was used to meeting in the advertising world in which she worked.

At first she doubted their compatibility. Although she was quite flattered by the fact that he always preferred to smooch rather than to talk and to go for intimate candle-lit dinners rather than to large, noisy parties, she was by nature a social creature. Those parties, which almost went with the job, had always seemed like an enjoyable diversion to her, and after a hard day at the office, when she was tense and wound up, she often found conversation more relaxing than a cuddling session on the sofa. But Ken was very sweet. He was devoted to her, and he was persistent. Gradually their affair deepened into a serious relationship. Diane's friends were delighted to see her so settled; Ken constantly told her that his whole world revolved around her; and slowly Diane's fears began to dissolve.

The cracks began to appear after they had been together for nearly two years. Diane describes what went wrong: 'Ken is a lovely guy, and in many ways he is my dream man. But in one respect we were completely unsuited: emotionally, he is a baby. At social occasions he would hover about me, looking as if he'd cry if I so much as talked to another man. At home he would cross-question me about everything I'd been doing, feeling, thinking – it was as if he wanted to own every part of me, inside and out. And discussing it made it worse. The more I'd struggle to assert my independence, the tighter he'd try to hold me, so to speak.

'I bumped into Andy one day. We'd had an affair a few years before. Nothing serious – it had ended with our just drifting apart. When Andy asked me how things were going with the boyfriend he'd heard about, something in me just snapped and it all came pouring out. I think it was something to do with his being like me, an independent, easy-going sort of person, and I knew he'd understand how much I couldn't stand to lose my freedom. It really helped to talk about things with him. And now I know for sure that, even though I know how hard he'll take it, I've got to make the break with Ken.

Whether things develop again between Andy and me, only
time will tell.'

Profile

The dominant Cosmo does not mind clinging tendencies in
her man; she certainly prefers them to bullying. However,
there are limits to how much clinging she can stand. She likes
to feel she's an independent agent.

A Clinger likes a Cosmo. She's assertive and reliable. If the
relationship lasts, it makes him feel secure. However, her
independence is liable to be experienced by him as abandonment even when he knows, rationally, that it's nothing of the
sort. This is what creates the problems for the Cosmo: the
irrationality of his clinging, the fact that she has no intention
of leaving him high and dry. Faced with the clinging day in,
day out, she may feel he needs to be shown she's not his
nanny and may deliberately try to wean him off her – which,
of course, only makes him more nervy.

At its most vulnerable the couple looks like this:

	Partner 1	Partner 2
Sexual personality type	Clinger	Cosmo
Second tendency	Big Boy	Splitter
Third tendency	Donor	Bully

The incompatible values and style of aggression of a Big
Boy–Cosmo pairing create a rumbling thunder that every so
often breaks out as a full-scale storm. He seems very contrary: as a Big Boy he insists on being seen as a strong,
independent person; as a Clinger he is the opposite, a bundle
of nerves and irrational fears. When they clash on values, she
is in a strong position to get her way. She points out the
contradictions in him, and he daren't fight back for fear of
abandonment. She may get quite a kick out of tormenting a
Big Boy in this way, but sooner or later she gets sick of it. A
Wimp comes along, and as she has a Splitter second tendency, she goes for him. She's had enough of the Big Boy's
antics and wants a maturer man.

At its least vulnerable this relationship can be stable and satisfying:

	Partner 1	Partner 2
Sexual personality type	Clinger	Cosmo
Second tendency	Wimp	Clinger
Third tendency	Splitter	Donor

Since both are prone to a fear of abandonment (as Clingers), they understand each other. They probably love each other deeply. The sex is good: varied, exciting and expressive of emotion. They share values and enjoy each other's interests. If the relationship continues over many years, their clinging will reduce in intensity because they make each other feel secure. They can talk problems out and find ways to be helpful without having to be told.

Only a Wimp with a Snatcher second tendency has any chance of breaking them up. It's not a relationship that's looking for a rock to crash into. Only in exceptional circumstances, such as immediately after the death of a parent or a reverse like getting the sack, is this couple likely to be in disarray. At such times a clever and sensitive Snatcher has an outside chance of persuading one of them that the grass is greener elsewhere.

CLINGER AND BIG BOY

Position in league: **Twenty-sixth**
Estimated proportion of this type of couple that has affairs: **45%**
Most likely unfaithful: **Big Boy**
Most likely third party: **Little Princess**

Case history

Hilary, the faithful Clinger
Ross, the unfaithful Big Boy
Gemma, the third-party Little Princess

Ross met Hilary when she was on the rebound from a disastrous marriage and a messy divorce. The shock of discovering her husband's adultery and the humiliation of the divorce were perhaps doubly hard for her to bear, reminding her as they did of her parents' acrimonious divorce. Ross's first impression of Hilary was of a wounded wild animal, fiercely defensive in her grief. It took him many months of patient courtship to win her trust and convince her that he was genuine in his desire to look after her. But his patience was rewarded, for when Hilary did eventually put her trust in him, her commitment to him was total. Other men might have found Hilary's devotion almost alarming in its intensity. But Ross too had always been passionate in his involvements, the sort of boy who would defend to the death anything from a stray puppy to a bullied schoolfellow, and he was far from put off by Hilary's expectations of absolute fidelity.

Gemma was an old schoolfriend of Hilary's, with whom she had little in common aside from the fact that they had both married and divorced at roughly the same time and, as a result, had kept in touch over the years. Hilary's new-found happiness annoyed Gemma. She had always considered herself the more attractive and the brighter of the two, and to see Hilary now with a good-looking, devoted husband was almost too much to bear when she was still single and frustrated. Besides, she rather fancied Ross herself.

She made more of a point now of keeping in contact with Hilary. So when Hilary was called from her home to look after her mother who was convalescing after an operation, it seemed only natural for Gemma to offer to keep Ross company and to help him with the housework.

One night, after she had prepared Ross a particularly lavish dinner, and they were enjoying a glass of brandy in the living-room, Gemma made her move. Ross was taken completely unawares, and perhaps because of the effect of the alcohol he offered no resistance. Ross will never know exactly what would have happened if the telephone had not rung at that moment. It was Hilary – it was almost as if her love for him and her jealousy had given her second sight into what was happening. The mood was broken, and Ross came to his senses.

Hilary will never know how close she came to having a second adulterous husband. And Ross understands full well that a blow like that could destroy her faith in humanity once and for all.

Profile

The Big Boy is happy to tolerate clinging tendencies in his woman, though if she is impossibly dependent on him, it can put him off. He cherishes his independence and doesn't want to receive anxious phone calls from his lover asking when he's going to be home.

The Big Boy's forcefulness makes the Clinger feel stable and confident and, over many years, will reduce her insecurity, making her less of a Clinger. His need for freedom of action will always cause her anxiety, though, which may irritate the Big Boy, who has no plan to leave her. At worst, he may finally be driven away from her by the Clinger cycle of dependence, assertion of freedom by partner, fear and more intense clinging.

At its most vulnerable the Clinger–Big Boy couple looks like this:

	Partner 1	*Partner 2*
Sexual personality type	Clinger	Big Boy
Second tendency	Cosmo	Splitter
Third tendency	Donor	Bully

The incompatible Big Boy–Cosmo combination creates trouble from the start. As a Cosmo she is strong and independent; as a Clinger she is fearful and nervous. When they clash he generally gets his way, and she retreats in fear of abandonment. Sooner or later a Little Princess makes a bid for him –

and succeeds. The Splitter in him responds to the new challenge: 'a real woman'.

At its least vulnerable this relationship is loving and rewarding:

	Partner 1	*Partner 2*
Sexual personality type	Clinger	Big Boy
Second tendency	Little Princess	Clinger
Third tendency	Splitter	Donor

Since both are Clingers, they offer each other sympathetic support. They are affectionate and see eye to eye about most issues. Their confidence in each other grows over the years.

Only a Little Princess with a Snatcher second tendency can threaten the relationship and then only at a time of special stress.

BIG BOY AND LITTLE PRINCESS

Position in league: **Twenty-seventh**

Estimated proportion of this type of couple that has affairs: **35%**

Most likely unfaithful: **The partner with Splitter tendencies**

Most likely third party: **Dominance-compatible Snatcher**

Case history

Sally, the faithful Little Princess
Benny, the unfaithful Big Boy
Jemima, the third-party Snatcher

Ten years into their marriage Sally's and Benny's life had settled into a satisfying pattern – not a rut but a mutually pleasing routine.

Benny: 'During the week we were happy to stay in, make

sure the kids got their homework done, relax and take it as it comes. At weekends we'd go to the beach, which is only fifteen minutes away in the car. Of course, our sex life wasn't the same as when we first met – both of us were too tired in the week mostly. But we'd have lots of time for that on Saturdays and Sundays.'

Into this settled existence came Jemima, the daughter of a distant acquaintance of Benny.

'When she first got the job in our office her dad rang me to ask if I'd keep an eye on her. Which is what I did, and not a roving eye either. She caused quite a stir when she first arrived. She was seventeen. She has long blonde hair that goes down to her waist. She stands very upright. Her skin looks like the wall of a newly painted, cream-coloured room. She smells crisp and fresh.

'She's a bit remote when you first meet her, but from little things she says you can tell she's an honest, affectionate, easy-going girl. She hasn't had too many problems in her life, as she is so pretty and uncomplicated. But she's not stupid either.

'After about two months she started dating my assistant, who was a couple of years older than her. It was very nice to see young love flourishing. Sometimes we'd all go for a drink after work. When she and Derek split up she was very sad about it. It affected her work, and one day I took her aside and asked if there was anything I could do. She started crying and I put my arm round her. To cheer her up I asked her out for a drink.'

Jemima: 'He was kind to me, and so at the end I asked if we could have another drink some time. He looked a bit taken aback and made a joke of it. But we often used to meet over a drink after that. I started dressing to please *him*, not Derek, and I suddenly began to get over Derek. The trouble was getting Benny to take me seriously.

'Then came my big chance. He was ill at home and the boss told me to go round there with some invoices that needed checking urgently. He was in bed . . .'

Benny: 'I hadn't made love like that for years. I fought the impulse to do it again, but I couldn't resist. After about three or four months, however, I began to realize the risk I was running. I love Sally, and I couldn't hurt her like this. It was terribly selfish. Thank goodness, Jemima understood when I told her it had to finish. I don't think I'd ever do anything like that again.'

Profile

Shared values, compatible styles of aggression and sexual compatibility provide a very solid foundation for this couple. Infidelity does not occur except in a small minority of cases where both have Bully second tendencies: rows blow up that can lead to revenge infidelity, but even then rarely does it destroy the whole relationship.

Both partners are reasonably stable, whatever their second tendencies. This makes them far less prone to irrational fantasies about the other. The confusion and misunderstanding that characterizes partners who are incompatible on the lust or insecurity dimension in mercifully absent.

In and out of bed, they share the same ideas. She believes a woman should stick up for her man, and he takes pleasure in his displays of forceful masculinity.

To make any headway with this couple a Snatcher needs to be very compatible on the dominance dimension and very lucky. For example, if the Big Boy has a Splitter second tendency, the Snatcher must be a Little Princess with at least as much to offer as the existing partner. The Big Boy is not going to be easily distracted. The Snatcher will have to pick the right moment – straight after the birth of a child, for example. If the relationship is three or four years old, chances are that the Splitter's lust for his partner has waned. Timely and cunning intervention by the Snatcher may get him off the straight and narrow and into her bed.

Likewise a Little Princess Splitter will take careful handling if she is already with a Big Boy. Maybe he lacks something. Looks? Power? Status? Wealth? Sense of humour? If so, after a few years she will be vulnerable to a wily Snatcher who is able to supply what is missing. Obviously he needs to pick the week her husband or lover is away on business, but it will take more than that: he's got to divine precisely what she feels is lacking and make a good job of supplying it. It may take a lot of acting and many lies.

WIMP AND COSMO

Position in league: **Twenty-eighth**
Estimated proportion of this type of couple that has affairs: **35%**
Most likely unfaithful: **The partner with Splitter tendencies**
Most likely third party: **Dominance-compatible Snatcher**

Case history

Diana, the faithful Cosmo
Gerry, the unfaithful Wimp
Tom, the third-party Big Boy

Gerry reached the age of 26 without ever having a proper adolescence. He'd worked very hard as a youth to get his engineering qualifications, and as a goalkeeper of unusual gifts he'd put his lithe, athletic body to good use in stopping many a goal both at university and, later, for his factory's team.

Gerry: 'In my teens I kept my nose in my books. Football was my only real indulgence. When I met Di at university, she was the first woman I'd ever really been close to. I had three brothers: ours had been a very male household.

'Di introduced me to sex, really. She was very knowledgeable – miles ahead of me. But then she was three years older.'

Diana: 'I suppose it's obvious now that he was getting

more and more stuck in his ways, but I didn't see that when I met him. He was old before his time, prematurely middle-aged. We'd been married about eighteen months, and he was already a creature of habit. But I liked the continuity, and we got on well – no rows or fundamental disagreements. I first realized he was changing when he started staying out late.'

Gerry: 'Tom is a fine striker of the ball – he's got brilliant timing. He scored a record number of goals in 1983 for our team. He works out in a gym, and after one game he suggested I come along too.

'At the gym there's a massage sauna. After the work-out you slump in the steam and give and get a massage. Normally massages were only of the back, but one evening, very calmly and firmly, he told me to roll over and started massaging my chest. I complied, though I was a bit worried. I couldn't look him in the eye afterwards and stopped going to the gym. But something took me back, and it went on from there.'

Profile

This couple is usually rocked only by Splitter and/or Donor second tendencies. So long as neither goes off sex because of these, infidelity occurs only in a few cases, when both are Bullies. Here rows may prompt infidelity, but the relationship rarely crumbles as a consequence.

Whatever their second tendencies, the Wimp and the Cosmo are generally confident in each other and suffer from little confusion about motives or what the other gets up to when they are apart.

In bed they each enjoy the fact that the other is different. He relishes her forcefulness, and he is her idea of a real man – he doesn't go in for aggressive displays of masculinity. At all times he's flexible and caring, and he *listens* to her.

They do not compete. They are amused by, and critical of, the same things in other people. If they spend the evening out with a Little Princess–Big Boy couple, they secretly communicate their disdain for conventional behaviour. When the Big Boy pays for his girl, they are proud of the fact that, as a

Wimp–Cosmo couple, they go Dutch. They're independent, separate people who don't want to be molly-coddled in social situations. If the Cosmo takes sides against the Wimp, he won't hold it against her. They don't think of each other as possessions. They respect each other and savour their different ways.

It's not easy for a Snatcher to break in. At its most vulnerable the Lust dimension is the key to this couple. After two or three years the Splitter in this combination begins to be less keen on sex. At times he or she finds the partner undesirable. It's then that the Snatcher is in with a chance, and the regular partner's Donor behaviour is bound to mean that opportunity knocks at some point. However, the Snatcher must be patient and wait for the right moment. An ill-judged comment or a poorly timed lunge will destroy all chances. Guilt and apprehension will quickly overwhelm the Splitter. The Snatcher will also have to analyse carefully what is missing in the relationship. Perhaps the Wimp has occasional outbursts of Big Boy behaviour and would be susceptible to a display of Little Princess qualities; maybe the Cosmo occasionally wants more of a challenge than her Wimp. Both may yearn for a socially more powerful partner. But on the whole it's hard to get between these two for any length of time.